D0385704

Praise for *Indispensable!*

"David Cottrell and Robert Nix once again prove that common sense can lead to great things. *Indispensable!* is a little book full of big ideas that can be understood and applied by anyone—anyone, that is, who really wants to increase their value, their respectability, and the likelihood they will be promoted. Read this book and take the first step above average to Indispensable!"

> Ken Blanchard, coauthor of *The One Minute Manager®* and *Trust Works!*

"You can become indispensable! Follow the simple approach outlined in this book to rise above the competition for your next promotion."

> Paul Spiegelman, bestselling author and founder of BerylHealth, recognized as the #2 Best Place to Work in America

"You need to be indispensable, and David Cottrell and Robert Nix explain exactly how to do it. Their straightforward advice comes from experience, and the process they teach works. If you want to get ahead at work and become a better person in the process, this book is for you."

> Mark Sanborn, author of *The Fred Factor* and *You Don't Need a Title to Be a Leader*

"*Indispensable!* is a powerful guide for all who want to become Indispensable within their organizations."

> Marshall Goldsmith, author of *What Got You Here Won't Get You There* and recognized as the #1 Most Influential Leadership Thinker in the World

"In a disposable business environment, Cottrell and Nix provide the antidote: becoming Indispensable. Their principles and skills on how character, performance, and great habits interface are a must-have. I highly recommend this book."

> John Townsend, organizational consultant and coauthor of the bestseller *Boundaries*

"Once again, David Cottrell, along with Robert Nix, has written a great book! This time it's on how to be Indispensable! This terrific book is easy to read and practical for everyday business, no matter what your business might be."

Garry Kinder, CEO, Kinder Brothers International

"This book is a powerful, detailed guide on how employees and organizations can become more successful. Everyone needs to read *Indispensable!*"

Greg Henslee, President and CEO, O'Reilly Auto Parts

"This book should become an 'Indispensable' part of your business library. The wise guidance outlined within *Indispensable!* is a great road map for anyone looking to move up in any organization."

Lorraine Grubbs, former Director of Employment, Southwest Airlines and author of *Lessons in Loyalty*

"Whether you are trying to get promoted or own a business that needs motivated and promotable associates, *Indispensable!* is for you. Read this book and follow the principles. It will help you become a better employee, peer, and leader."

Pat Williams, Orlando Magic cofounder and Senior Vice President and author of *Coach Wooden's Greatest Secret*

"David Cottrell and Robert Nix have written an engaging book that will inspire you to rise above the crowd. *Indispensable!* was written to remind us that what we do, or fail to do, today will determine our future opportunities. In our modern workplace a stagnant sea of sameness and mediocrity is everywhere. *Indispensable!* will help you to determine the unique abilities you have and to develop them into increased effectiveness. Cottrell and Nix will teach you specific traits and skills that will get you noticed as a productive and committed team player ready for advancement. Each chapter ends with a powerful section titled

'Take Action' that will help you to apply the key concepts of the book. Perhaps most important, *Indispensable!* will help you to be prepared for maximum achievement when opportunities arise in your future. If you're looking for a book that can help you to stand out among the crowd, this is the one, and it is truly Indispensable."

> Greg L. Thomas, founder of we LEAD Incorporated and
> Leadership Excellence, Ltd.

"Cottrell and Nix's easy-to-follow insight and action plans for quickly becoming indispensable to your organization, coupled with your own intuition—often considered the sum total of your life experiences—will undoubtedly prepare you for the success and boundless opportunities that your career has in store."

> Kip Tindell, Chairman and CEO, The Container Store,
> named one of *Fortune* magazine's 100 Best Companies to
> Work For 14 years in a row

"David Cottrell's *Monday Morning Leadership* was a hit out of the park, and *Indispensable!* is a shot heard around the world. This is a must-read for everyone seeking to enter the C-suites as well as those with their sights on the next level of the leadership ladder."

> Jack F. Smalley, SPHR, Director HR Learning & Development,
> Express Employment Professionals

"*Indispensable!* contains so many practical observations and useful ideas it is like having a seasoned management mentor help you get the most out of your career."

> Eric Severson, Executive VP of Sales, Pearson Education

"This book gives you a step-by-step formula to make yourself valuable and then 'Indispensable,' saving you years of hard work in reaching higher levels of both income and success."

> Brian Tracy, author of *Earn What You're Really Worth*

"Putting Robert and David's four tests into place (talent, values, desire, and courage) allows individuals to take the steps necessary to make themselves 'Indispensable!' in the workplace. It is a great primer for those reexamining their occupation or those just beginning their career. Talent Plus agrees with the authors: 'It is your responsibility to understand your talents, values, and desires and then develop the courage to move forward.'"

Kimberly Rath, President, Talent Plus, recognized as one of the Achievers 50 Most Engaged Workplaces

Indispensable!

Indispensable!

Becoming the Obvious Choice
in Business and in Life

David Cottrell and
Robert Nix

New York   Chicago   San Francisco   Athens   London
Madrid   Mexico City   Milan   New Delhi
Singapore   Sydney   Toronto

1 2 3 4 5 6 7 8 9 0   DOC/DOC   1 9 8 7 6 5 4 3

ISBN   978-0-07-182939-7
MHID   0-07-182939-3

e-ISBN   978-0-07-182940-3
e-MHID   0-07-182940-7

Library of Congress Cataloging-in-Publication Data

Cottrell, David.
Indispensable!: becoming the obvious choice in business and in life/by David Cottrell and Robert Nix.
   pages cm
   ISBN 978-0-07-182939-7 (alk. paper)
   ISBN 0-07-182939-3 (alk. paper)
   1. Promotions.   2. Career development.   I. Title.
   HF5549.5.P7C67 2014
   650.14—dc23   2013012564

McGraw-Hill Education books are available at special quantity discounts to use as premiums and sales promotions or for use in corporate training programs. To contact a representative, please visit the Contact Us pages at www.mhprofessional.com.

To every man there comes in his lifetime that special moment when he is tapped on the shoulder and offered the chance to do a very special thing.

What a tragedy if that moment finds him unprepared or unqualified for the work which would be his finest hour.
—WINSTON CHURCHILL

This book is dedicated to every person who has the courage to prepare for his or her finest hour and become Indispensable!

Contents

Introduction

Becoming Indispensable Begins Now

in•dis•pens•able 1: not subject to being set aside or neglected 2: absolutely necessary : essential
Merriam-Webster's Collegiate Dictionary, Eleventh Edition

"How can I become indispensable—absolutely necessary and essential—to my organization?" "How can I earn my next promotion?" Aren't those questions that we have all asked? After all, we want to earn more, learn more, and be more secure in our career.

The fact is that the selection process for promoting someone into a new opportunity or deciding who to retain during cutbacks does not begin the day the position becomes available or when cutbacks are needed. No, people are being evaluated for new opportunities long before a new position is even conceived. You see, you are interviewing and competing today and tomorrow and next week too. Whether you know it or not, decisions about your future could be based on how you handle a situation, interact, and represent the organization in your job today. Managers rarely offer greater opportunities to someone and then expect that person to suddenly appear different, more capable, more focused. Most often, managers promote people or retain personnel based on what they already know about those people.

This book is designed to guide you to prepare for your next opportunity—right now—and help you become indispensable to your current employer. It is not for those who believe they are entitled to something or anything. Nor is it for those who are satisfied with the status quo. Tomorrow will not necessarily be better unless you begin your preparation to become indispensable today.

The strategies presented in this book are for those willing to honestly reflect on their circumstances and their daily habits—and make changes. It is for those who want to break through, do things differently, take action, challenge life, and control their own destiny. It is for those who understand that becoming indispensable for the next opportunity is a process of presenting and selling themselves and their abilities.

I have had the opportunity to work with thousands of people who sincerely desired to move up within their organization but did not know how to make it happen. Robert Nix has spent years in successful sales and in sales management. We have collaborated on this book to ensure that it provides a success path for everyone. It offers help to those searching for a career, looking to advance, or desiring to improve. It provides discussion topics and personal growth strategies that can benefit any person within any organization.

Follow the suggestions detailed in this book, and when the right time comes, it will be crystal clear to everyone that you are, indeed, Indispensable!

David Cottrell
Horseshoe Bay, Texas

SECTION ONE

Square One

*If you are going to fulfill your destiny, you gotta
get in the game, you gotta stay in the game,
and you gotta follow the game plan.*
—BILLY COX

CHAPTER 1

Escaping the Status Quo

This is like déjà vu all over again.
—YOGI BERRA

A four-by-six, brownish-gray cloth cubicle waits. It waits there … in the middle row, on the middle floor, in the middle of the building, in the middle of the street, in the middle of the city.

Perhaps it awaits you.

Somewhat sarcastically and with an underlying, embarrassed resentment, you call it your "achievement center." The outer walls look no different from the next cubicle with the exception of a nameplate announcing your location in a faceless crowd of other coworkers in the same cookie-cutter, four-by-six, brownish-gray cloth achievement centers. You have placed a mirror there, by your keyboard, to alert you when some quiet passerby stops to peer uncomfortably over your shoulder. Nothing you do or say is private. You know this from experience because you hear and smell more about the lives of your fellow cubicle coworkers than you desire.

Whether the sun shines, the wind blows, or the rain falls, you see only brief glimpses of the outside world. Along the precious landscape of windows are offices with doors, real desks, and even chairs for visitors. In these walled-off offices reside people who have somehow escaped their caste confinement in the brownish-gray modular workspaces. Now these office people watch the activities of the cubicle people and sometimes even close their walled-office doors and discuss with other walled-office people what they see … or don't see. Occasionally they discuss you.

Of course there are worse places to work than that four-by-six achievement center, and work experience is important for your future. But was it ever part of the vision you had about life? Was it your dream to be confined to a nondescript, cookie-cutter existence of sameness? Was it your goal to be one of many? Organizations need people in workspaces. It does not have to be you.

There is an answer. You can escape the cubicle.

*   *   *

Standing behind the counter, you watch the clock. The minimum wage challenges your willingness to work through an aching back, tired feet, and embarrassing uniforms. It is the third job you have had this year, and it bears little difference from the previous two. The door opens, electronics chime, and another customer enters—no smile and dragging an attitude. The manager just informed you it is time for your employee review. Looking around, suddenly everything appears in slow motion. Every day you have hoped something better would come along. All around you are fellow employees in the identical uniforms. In this introspective moment, you recognize that they have become your mirror. You speak like them, dress like them, complain like them, and earn like them. Their view of the future has become yours. You are jolted back to reality. A customer has spilled an industrial-sized vat of cola by the front door, and it is your responsibility to clean it up. The customer has walked away hurriedly, laughing and offering no remorse or assistance.

Of course there are worse places to work than behind a counter, and interacting with the public is valuable experience. But was it ever part of the vision you had about life? Was it your dream to wear a smock and take orders from everyone? Was it ever your hope that next year you could receive a $0.50-per-hour raise? Companies need people in smocks fulfilling requests. It does not have to be you.

There is an answer. You can escape the counter.

* * *

A business struggles. Your associates' attitude is to put in the hours of eight to five or preferably less. Employees push the limits of casual day. Delays in IT are part of the daily employee banter and associated eye-rolling. Customer Service isn't. Managers gather off-site to rate the staff and discuss financial cutbacks, and they strategically attempt to deflect blame. But no one stops to consider that the staff, the product, and the work effort most often reflect the attitude, the personality, and the drive of those who lead. Was the original business model to be inefficient, late to market, and mired in the lack of creative solutions? To employ a workforce of unmotivated task zombies? Many organizations are mired in poor performance and little vision. It does not have to be yours.

There is an answer. Your organization can achieve more!

* * *

You can escape the status quo by being the very best right where you are. To be the very best, you have to look, act, and sell like the very best.

You may not believe that you are in sales. You may think that salespeople are those pests calling you on the phone, bugging you at the mall, and deceiving you at the car lot. You may not even like salespeople, and you attempt to dodge all interaction with them. You may tire of their "May I help you" when you know they actually mean "Can you help me by buying this?"

But whatever your work space (cubicle, counter, driver's seat, corner office), whatever your action (customer service rep, cook, driver, coach, programmer, manager, business owner), whatever your goals (more money, status, recognition, security), and whatever your hopes … you are selling yourself every day, in every encounter.

Unknowingly, you may be selling mediocrity. You may be selling a lack of interest and passion or a critical attitude. Whether you believe, intend, or want to … you are selling. Every day, every meeting, every casual encounter with upper management, every interaction with fellow employees, customers, delivery people … you are selling. Whether you are a business owner, hourly employee, entrepreneur, jobseeker, doctor, new employee, or tenured employee … you are selling.

Of course it's not fair. There were no classes in school on selling. You studied accounting, programming, business, or maybe even psychology. Your company has not sent you to sales seminars, training courses, or even recommended a book on sales. Your employer is busy teaching you how to do a task, a procedure, a responsibility, a service, a report, a reoccurring set of mundane activities. And you have responded, perhaps even excelled … there in your achievement center or behind that counter. But no one has taught you how to sell yourself.

Never fear, the news is GOOD! Here is the secret. Stop and look around. All of those cubicles have people doing their daily tasks, hoping for a 2 percent increase in pay, who just like you simply do not realize they are selling. They are consumed with their daily routine and responsibilities. They are selling mediocrity, without knowing that they have control over their own future. They are successfully selling that they are exactly where they belong.

There is an old joke about a couple of hikers on a forest trail. Suddenly a hungry bear spots them in the path. Recognizing the danger, the hikers turn to escape. One hiker stops and fumbles through their backpack, frantic to put on a pair of running shoes. The other hiker stops to look back and yells, "What are you doing? Even with those athletic shoes, you will never outrun the bear." The track-shoed hiker responds, "I don't have to outrun the bear. I simply have to outrun you!"

Now you know whom you will be competing with for your next opportunity … the people around you. They may be your friends and coworkers. But they are also your competition to a better position, more status, more money, a better office, or whatever your goals and hopes are. You will not betray them by positioning yourself and achieving more. You betray yourself by accepting their standards. If you act like your competition, talk like your competition, look like your competition, have the same attitude as your competition, then guess how you will be viewed in comparison to your competition?

How are you selling yourself? Have you succumbed to the philosophies and negative examples that surround you? The reality is that we are not dramatically different in degrees of intelligence or competence. We are more often victims of our own expectations and efforts. We sell ourselves short. A Gallop study published in July 2011 revealed that only 27 percent of U.S. workers are engaged with their employment.[1]

"Engaged" means actively committed. Only 27 percent. For you, this should be good news. The competition is small.

A popular word used to describe the 73 percent majority of today's workforce is "disengaged." It's an interesting way to describe someone—detached, disconnected, cut off. Who wants to spend the majority of their waking hours that way? Why would people consciously choose to be disengaged? Don't fall into the same trap others are in. You are the driver of your success. You can do better!

This book's goal is to help you learn how to better sell yourself. You can become more. Whatever your goals or circumstances, people will notice a change. It is not about bragging, talking louder, or being a jerk. It is about illustrating how good you actually are, regardless of your past history, age, economic condition, or your hardships. Whatever your definition of success is, if you want to become indispensable, your success will be determined by action, commitment, and effort.

Most people are satisfied with mediocrity. Let that sink in. Most people are *satisfied* with mediocrity. They may want more, but they are not willing to challenge themselves and escape the valley of mediocrity.

Those stuck in mediocrity have accepted their roles and given up. Excuses are easier than honestly looking within. Excuses are trial balloons that we send up, checking to see if anyone is accepting. When our excuses are not challenged and they are accepted by those around us, then those excuses start to develop our self-view of our internal worth, and over time that view becomes a reality. The white flag comes out ... we have surrendered. We have become the disengaged. We live in the valley of mediocrity.

Success, happiness, attitude, and effort are all choices. Your choice. In this life, everyone will face hardships, bad news, health issues, unforeseen obstacles, insults, bias, and other devastating events. Everyone. How people react to these moments in time is what separates the successful from the trapped. The reaction you have to any issue is your choice. You can choose to be depressed, to give up, and to assume that all is against you. You can also choose to fight through it, to survive, to excel, to smile, to beat the odds, to believe. You can choose to be passionate with your life. Even if you do not yet know what your life's mission will ultimately be, now is the time to prepare to become indispensable.

This does not mean that you will not face obstacles or that you will win every difficulty. It means you do not have to be defined by the difficulty. You do not have to give fear the authority to dictate your future. Something or someone is going to direct your future. Why not make it you?

Becoming indispensable is not easy. Most folks will quit before they begin. Others will give up along the way. Some will deny they need to change. But the people who are all talk and full of excuses are easy competition to those determined to achieve more.

Are you willing to become indispensable?

Take Action

You have probably seen Olympic athletes visualize their maneuvers, strategies, and races. Visualization is a powerful tool. It provides them with a rehearsal in their brain for what they are about to do with their body. After visualizing a spectacular performance, they replay live the performance they have already seen.

Visualization will work for you too.

What if you spent time considering what you will do tomorrow, what you will say, how you will act, what you will wear, where you will go, how you will position yourself? Visualize yourself being successful and indispensable. Think about it: How would the most successful people you know look, act, speak, and interact with those around you? Visualize how they would respond when they are faced with a difficult challenge. What if you mentally practiced handling situations similarly—that is, with a positive attitude and manner?

What would happen is … you would be better prepared for anything that could happen. As you read this book, visualize yourself incorporating changes in your life. Think about how you will interact with others in various situations and how you will maintain a positive and dynamic attitude.

The first step to becoming indispensable is to see yourself as that person and to act as though you are indispensable already. Beginning today, act on your positive vision and begin separating yourself from your competition.

CHAPTER 2

Reality Check

Know thyself.
—SOCRATES

Not every person is cut out for every job. And that's OK. For some, being promoted can be a disastrous career step. Many times the best salesperson is promoted into sales management. Within a month, or even sooner, that same "best salesperson" has created nothing but chaos for that once crack sales team, customers, and everybody else. An excellent nurse may not be a good nursing supervisor. An outstanding insurance agent may not be a good corporate trainer. You get the picture. In fact, that outstanding salesperson, nurse, or agent would much rather be doing anything other than giving performance reviews.

Is it your manager's responsibility to prevent this disaster from happening to you?

No. It is your responsibility to understand your talents, values, and desires and then develop the courage to move forward. In addition, it is your responsibility to evaluate how these elements fit the requirements of the position you may be seeking. If you find that there is a conflict within any of those areas, you are destined to be miserable. And, chances are, you will not be successful. The most rewarding opportunities are those that utilize your unique talents and provide you enjoyment and fulfillment—without conflicting with your values.

There are four tests you can give yourself to determine if you should pursue the next opportunity. Does the new position pass the talent, values, desire, and courage tests? Here's how you can tell.

THE TALENT TEST

> *Don't paint stripes on your back if you're not a zebra.*
> *Focus on building upon your unique abilities.*
> —LEE J. COLAN

Everyone has talents. These talents vary from person to person, but everyone has areas of excellence. The key to job satisfaction and long-term success is discovering what your talents are and becoming the best at putting these talents to work.

Your greatest area of expertise may be in your current job—there is nothing wrong with that. If this is the case, and you are reaching your goals, great. But if you have talents that exist beyond your current position, you're cheating yourself and your employer by not pursuing advancement.

However, a word of caution: don't confuse talent with desire.

Talent is being naturally gifted in a certain area. It may be writing, selling, auditing, human relations, nursing … whatever.

Desire is completely different. It is something you would like to happen.

For instance, I would love to be a professional golfer. I have that burning desire, and I am willing to work 14 hours a day to make it happen. The problem is that I'm just an OK golfer. And frankly I do not think I could ever make a living playing golf, no matter how much I wanted it or how hard I tried. I would be thrilled to be on the golf tour, but that will never happen. I assure you, people would not pay to see me play golf.

What I realize is that my talents are in other areas, and it's in those areas that I need to spend my energy. I can still enjoy golf as a hobby, but I can't fool myself into thinking that it will ever be more than a hobby.

So, where are your areas of excellence? What activities are seldom boring, even when you are doing the same thing over and over? What do others say that you are especially good at doing? What comes naturally to you? What skills feel good and comfortable when you use them?

Discover those areas, and focus on finding the right place—the right job—that relies on them—your "talents," your gifts.

THE VALUES TEST

> *There is no pillow as soft as a clear conscience.*
> —JOHN WOODEN

You probably know more than one extremely intelligent, success-ful person who is totally miserable. Their misery exists because their job clashes with their personal values. Maybe the job requires constant travel and time away from family. Or they have to work a schedule that keeps them away from participating in and enjoying their kids' activities. The money may be great—but those people may be under constant stress because of their desire for more time at home.

Somewhere along the way, you will probably face a tough decision: Are you willing to sacrifice your personal values for short-term gain? Listen to yourself. Deep down, how do you feel about the situation? If money or prestige was not involved, would you be pursing this opportunity?

Before pursuing your next position—that next step up—know yourself and your values. Then check out what the position requires, and make sure that it won't create a "values clash." You may have to make trade-offs in some areas, but at least take the time to fully understand what's involved in this give-and-take process. If the promotion is not right for you, for your sake and the sake of your organization, let it pass, and wait until your right opportunity appears.

THE DESIRE TEST

> *When work, commitment, and pleasure all become*
> *one and you reach that deep well where passion lives,*
> *nothing is impossible.*
> —ANONYMOUS

"Do I really want this promotion?" Only you know the answer.

If that next job is something that fits into your long-range plan, go for it. If it does not help you achieve your personal goals, let others pursue it. You can't force yourself to like broccoli—you know yourself.

There is a price tag on every job. The price may involve taking time out to develop new skills. It may also contain a component that raises the "fear of the unknown." It may put you in the position of becoming the manager of current associates, or it may put you in other types of uncomfortable situations.

The message here? Take the time to evaluate the price you may be called upon to pay, and match it up with your desires, values, and talents.

If you have a talent that coincides with your values, and you have a desire for that next job—go for it with all you have. However, if the results of any of the three tests—talent, values, and desire—are not positive, pass on this opportunity, and continue preparing for the job in which you will be more successful.

THE COURAGE TEST

Man cannot discover new oceans unless he has the
courage to lose sight of the shore.
—ANDRÉ GIDE

Charlie Jones is a former sportscaster who covered several Olympic Games in his long and successful career. At the 1996 games in Atlanta, he was assigned to announce the rowing, canoeing, and kayaking events—a situation that left him less than thrilled since the events were broadcast at 7 a.m. and the venue was an hour's drive from Atlanta. It was not exactly a prestige assignment for a Hall of Fame sportscaster.

What Jones discovered, however, was that it ended up being one of the most memorable sports events in his career. He gained a chance to understand the mental workings of these Olympic athletes. Preparing for the broadcast, Jones interviewed the rowers and asked them what they would do in case of rain, strong winds, or breaking an oar. The response was always the same: "That's outside my boat."

After hearing the same answer again and again, Jones realized that these Olympic athletes had a remarkable focus. In their attempt to win an Olympic medal, he wrote, "They were interested only in what they could control—and that was what was going on inside their boat." Everything else was beyond their control and not worth expending any mental energy or attention that would distract them from their ultimate goal. Jones says that this insight made the event "by far the best Olympics of my life."

We all have moments when we need to redirect our efforts "inside the boat" to keep ourselves focused.

There are some factors over which you have no choice, like how tall you are. There are other factors over which you have some control, like how much you weigh. There are still other factors over which you have total control, like your hair style or general grooming.

Being indispensable demands that you exhibit the courage to decide to spend time and resources on the factors that are within your control. Take control over what you can, and accept that some things are beyond your control, but do the best you can with them. Never give up improving the things that you can control.

People who lose courage may give up. Others may be paralyzed with fear. Some may talk but not act. They may be hiding and peeking around the corners to see if anyone believes the excuses they offer. Any of these excuses sound familiar?

"I just like to be comfortable."

"I don't care what people say or think of me."

"One day, when I have time, I will …"

"I like to be unique."

"Everybody else does …"

Insecurity leads to excuse justification. It is natural and easier to offer excuses than it is to take the blame for failure. Excuse-laden people impact everyone they come into contact with—journey complete, circumstances accepted, go on without me.

The Indispensable person takes control over what he or she controls and moves forward without excuses.

Perhaps it is uncomfortable, but look inside you. Are you making any excuses? Are you trying to convince others that you dress the way you do because it is comfortable? Are you telling others that "looks do not matter to you" and then hope they believe you? Are you telling others you don't have enough time to …? Do you have the courage to zap the excuses and move forward?

Know this: everyone has insecurities, fears, and weaknesses. There will always be someone prettier or more handsome. There will always be someone smarter, wiser. There will always be someone funnier, wittier. There will be issues in your past that have created scars and fear.

Perhaps because of your past you are wearing a mask. Maybe a mask made of unusual clothing, edgy hairstyle, unhealthy weight, or lone wolf attitude. But whatever the past, whatever the insecurity, going forward is a choice. You get to choose what your attitude, actions, appearance, and goals for tomorrow are. It may take effort. It will take courage. It will involve change. But it is a choice! Every day you wake up, you have the choice. Your future may be compromised and detoured by misfortune, but your future does not have to be ravaged. You may not wish to acknowledge it to yourself, but difficulties are not unique to you. We all share hard times at some point.

Whatever "it" is in your way will only win if you allow it. If you need professional help to address your issues, then see a counselor or join a mentoring group. If you need encouragement, find someone who loves you. Others have faced similar and maybe even more challenging obstacles. Franklin D. Roosevelt was paralyzed, Beethoven was deaf, Stevie Wonder was born blind, and John McCain was an injured prisoner of war for over five years. No problem is unique to you. Others have faced "it" and overcome "it." You can too.

It takes courage to change from the known into the unknown. When you make a change of any kind, you are exiting a comfortable place and entering an area that could be the launching pad for you. Every time you go through an exit, whether it is job related or personal, you are making an entrance into a new opportunity. The only way for you to enter into the next level of your career is to exit the current level. That's what positive change does—it exits the status quo and enters into a new beginning.

The success of any change depends, in large measure, on your attitude about that change.

Henry Ford once said, "One of the great discoveries a man makes, one of his great surprises, is to find he can do what he was afraid he couldn't do." He was talking about exiting the comfortable and entering the uncomfortable.

You cannot move forward without having the courage to exit the familiar. Courage does not mean that you have no fear. Mark Twain defined courage as "resistance to fear, mastery of fear—not absence of fear." We walk forward along a path; fear is there too. We keep walking.

Most people think that the opposite of courage is cowardice. That is a good answer, but I think the best answer to the opposite of courage is conformity. Courage is having the guts and the heart to do things differently for the sake of progress. Improvement doesn't happen by taking the path of least resistance or conforming to the way things have always been done.

Have the courage to be the best you can be. Don't reflect to others that you don't care. If your dress, hygiene, attitude, or demeanor reflects apathy, do you think that builds confidence with those around you? If you do not care about yourself, then others, including your employers, will assume that you will not care about and manage, protect, and build their interests.

It is better to understand your weaknesses, acknowledge them, and deal with them than it is to mask them. The first thing to do is admit them. Perhaps only to yourself, but admit them. Write them down. Then you must decide. *Will* you alter them? Not *can* you alter them. You can. Will you? If you need help, will you seek it? The fear and fences that you have erected may not be overcome in a day, a week, or a year. But understand that the effort can begin today, this minute. Your choice. Do not let anyone or anything have controlling power over your attitude and actions.

You can do it! It is inside your boat. You can become Indispensable!

Take Action

What are your talents—your areas of expertise?

_____

_____

Does the position for which you aspire to be indispensable align with your talents?

Does the position you are seeking align with the values with which you have chosen to live your life?

Are you willing to pay the price to be indispensable?

What are the excuses that you have offered to convince yourself why you cannot achieve more? Be honest with yourself, and write them down.

_____

_____

Do you have the courage to eliminate those excuses so that you can earn your next promotion?

The Indispensable person takes action and stops making excuses.

CHAPTER 3

Establishing Your Path

If you don't know where you are going, you will
probably end up somewhere else.
—Lawrence J. Peter

Let the eye-rolling begin. Here comes a chapter on goal setting, and you have read it all before. You have heard all your life that goals are important and that you should set goals. But, for whatever reason, you may have never gotten around to setting meaningful goals for yourself.

Now things are different. It is time to pay attention and test the power of strategic goal setting because you have chosen to become indispensable.

All sports have some sort of goal. They also have coaches, strategies, clocks, and stats, and they keep score—otherwise sporting events would just be watching people exercise in public wearing matching costumes. However, once we get past the age of five, the tee-stand goes away, and we do not play just to enjoy our juice box after it is over. We play games to win. Why don't we do the same with our career and life?

Most people do not set goals of any kind. No tangible goals of any variety. Many of those who have goals do not write down or share their specific goals. They are interested in accomplishing them, but they are not committed to stating them clearly. Without writing and stating a specific, clear picture of what they want for themselves, they drift aimlessly.

Becoming indispensable begins with a crystal-clear understanding of what you are trying to accomplish.

If you want to reach your goal, you have to mentally see the goal and then physically write the goal. Just seeing is not good enough. Your goal has to be written in your handwriting. Writing down your goals will clarify what you are trying to accomplish. It marks the beginning of your commitment to accomplishing those goals.

Benjamin Franklin made a list of traits he either wanted to get rid of or wanted to cultivate. Then he graded himself on his progress or regression every day. Not yearly, weekly, or monthly, but every day. His question to himself was, "Did I get closer to accomplishing my goals, or did I lose ground today?" Franklin chose to be more than interested in accomplishing his goals. He was committed enough to his goals to take the time to measure his progress. He was committed enough to keep his goals in view, working in some way each day to take one step forward.

Writing down and measuring progress toward your goals is not "old school." It's your first step to accomplishing your dreams.

When my son, Michael, left home for college, he proudly announced that he had set his academic goal for his first semester. I had taught him all his life to be a goal setter, and he knew the importance of mentally creating a goal and then physically doing the necessary things to make the goal happen.

I asked him what his goal was for his first semester at Texas A&M. He would not tell me his goal—he said he had it under control—and I did not press him on the matter. I was not certain what his expectations were for himself. My expectations were that he would be involved, have a good time, adjust to being away from home, and not be on scholastic probation after his first semester.

When the semester was over, his transcript was mailed to him. He opened it, and his grade point average was 3.8. He then opened an envelope in which he had placed a sheet of paper where his goal was written to show me the goal he had set at the beginning of the semester. It was 3.8.

Coincidence? Maybe, but probably not. He was focused on a 3.8. He was more than interested in making it happen. He was committed to pay the price to make it happen. His goal was written everywhere: in his wallet, on his mirror, and everywhere he looked. Every day he measured and graded himself, striving for the 3.8 he would eventually achieve.

One irony of that story? I would have suggested that he set his goal lower for his first semester away at school. After all, he beat my own first-semester grade point average by a huge margin! But he set his own goal and was passionately committed to achieve HIS goal.

Written goals—personally set, continually visualized, and important enough to be worth paying the price for success—have a mysterious way of coming true.

If goals are so important, then why do people fail to set goals? I have observed that there are five major reasons:

- People simply don't understand the enormous and enabling power of goal setting.

- Others feel writing a goal is unnecessary—they think they can commit to a goal without writing it down. That is simply an excuse and not true. Commitment begins with clarity. Clarity begins with writing.

- Many expect to fail before they even get started, so why risk success?

- Some believe they have no control over life's challenges, so what is the use?

- Goals require people to exit their comfort zone.

Your goals are important to your future. Don't fall into the trap of justifying why you do not need to set goals. Becoming indispensable requires specific, personal, and measurable goals. They set your course and provide you with motivation. When you accomplish goals, you gain confidence and momentum.

What are your goals? If your answer is "I don't know," then you are going to get somewhere you don't know. And that may well be where you did not want to go—who knows ... maybe ... I'm not sure, I don't know, whatever.

The old you probably did not set goals. But the new you ... the person who is becoming indispensable ... needs to set goals. Set your goals in place, and go for them! Plan and set a course toward achieving more than you thought possible. Focusing and striving to reach goals that you define will diminish the negative and accentuate the positive. Don't let the negative attitude of others stop you. This is your time, your watch, and your life. Be the pilot of your destiny.

If you need some help, try some of the following questions that will help you get started:

What about yourself would you like to improve?

What do you need to do to improve your family life?

What would your dream job be?

Where do you want to be in five years?

What would you like to do to help others?

What would you like to learn?

Do you need to focus more on your faith?

What could you do to improve your health?

You don't have to share your goals with anyone if you're not ready—although it would help. Sharing your goals with a friend will help motivate you. Even more, that friendship could become a mutual accountability check point. But the primary person who needs to know your goals is you. Once you determine your specific goals, dwell on them. Write them down. Keep them visible. You may think writing them down is dumb. You may think that you will remember or it is a waste of your energy.

But don't turn another page without writing your goals. You can do it in a secret notebook, or you can write them for all to see, but write them. Real goals, real hopes. Establish short-term and long-term goals, and challenge yourself by becoming your best.

Grab an index card, notebook, or your smartphone, and write your goals. Go ahead right now. Think about what you really want to accomplish.

Now, at a minimum, every Sunday evening or Monday morning, read them. Start your week off working toward them. If you are a person who prays, then pray about them. If you are a person who keeps a diary, then write about them. If you are a person who sings, then sing about them. Whatever you do, know them, and think about them. If your goals change, then change them. But from now on, know where you're going. Be stubborn, be focused, and be motivated to reach your goals. The more clearly you understand your desired result, the better your chances are of visualizing and eventually accomplishing your goals. Success is rehearsed long before it "suddenly appears" for the Indispensable person.

OK, so you have your goals set. It may take you a year or the next 20 years to reach them. However, here is the important step that you may not have defined: What will you do today? To reach your dreams, the action starts today ... now. The action continues every day. Tomorrow is too late. Tomorrow often becomes part of some self-justified, excuse chant—"Tomorrow I will. Tomorrow I'm going to. Tomorrow I'll start." There are always tomorrows until there aren't. What will you do today to start and continue the process to reach your goals? What plans will you implement? Even if your goal is 20 years out, there are steps that need to be taken today.

If you want to become the Indispensable person, your goals must have an action plan that begins right now.

Take Action

Determine your goals, write your goals, and read your goals at least once a week, starting today. Don't worry if they sound too big. Whatever they are, what will you do today to begin the course?

Below is a path for you to follow that can change your life and career:

1. See It!

Envision the goal in your mind. Visualize it as a positive situation—what you want to happen rather than what you don't want to happen.

2. Feel It!

Write the goal on paper, and describe it in a positive, personal, and present tense. (For example: "I am a nonsmoker on June 18.")

Do a reality check by asking these questions:

- "Why do I want to achieve this goal?"
- "Do I desire this goal intensely?"
- "Is it achievable and realistic?"
- "Am I willing to pay the price to achieve the goal?"

3. Trust It!

Whom can you tell who will support you and hold you accountable?

4. Do It!

Make a plan:

- Identify where are you starting from: What is your current situation?

- Set a deadline date to accomplish the goal.

- Identify the obstacles to overcome.

- Determine whose help you will need to accomplish the goal.

- How are you going to accomplish the goal? List the specific activities required as well as the priority of the activities.

The Indispensable person establishes his or her path by becoming a champion goal achiever.

SECTION TWO

Look Like You Mean Business

*Behavior is a mirror in which everyone
displays his own image.*
—JOHAN WOLFGANG VAN GOETHE

CHAPTER 4

Reflecting What You Want Others to See

How we think shows through in how we act. Attitudes
are mirrors of the mind. They reflect thinking.
—David Joseph Schwartz

A salesman moved into a new town and met an old-timer as he was leaving the bank. "I'm new to your town. What are the people like here?" the salesman asked.

"What were the people like in the town you came from?" the old-timer asked in return.

"Well, they were glum and negative and always complaining, and their glasses were always half empty, never half full," the salesman replied.

"Hmmm," said the old-timer. "Sounds about like the people who live here."

31

A few weeks later, another person moved to the same town and met the same old-timer as he was leaving the same bank. "I'm new to your town. What are the people like here?" the newcomer asked.

"What were the people like in the town you came from?" the old-timer asked again.

"Well, they were wonderful. They worked together in the neighborhood, helped each other out, and were always there to support us during tough times. We're going to miss them now that we've moved," the newcomer replied.

"Hmmm," said the old-timer. "I think you will like it here. That sounds about like the people who live here."

The old-timer's message? If you want to be around people who are positive and enthusiastic and eager to live life, your attitude has to be the same. If you think the people around you are glum and negative, you probably need to check your attitude. It's probably glum and negative too.

If you want to be around happier people, choose to be happy yourself. It all starts with you. As an old farmer used to tell his children, "You can't change the fruit without changing the root." Our root is our attitude, and our fruit is how others see us.

There are few relationships more important to you than your relationship with what you see in the mirror. We love mirrors—in private. We spend hours of our lives, one-on-one, concocting our best reflection. We do our best to present an appearance that we are convinced represents us to the pinnacle of our physical abilities. And when additional advice or help is needed, there are products, techniques, magazines, and physicians willing to assist us, regardless of the challenge.

Mirrors are interesting. When you shop for athletic shoes, the mirrors are low, offering a glimpse of how those running shoes will look when we are challenging the turf. Forget support or comfort. Do they make us look athletic, fast, chic, successful ... even if we choose not to run?

When we buy sunglasses, we look into that little narrow mirror there on the store rack. Skip the UV protection, the polarization, the lens quality. We contort, squat, and look sideways, attempting to get a view of those shades on our face. Perhaps we can get a view of only one eye at a time. But do we look glamorous, cool, tough, and most of all mysterious?

There are mirrors everywhere. Compact mirrors, mirrors on the sun visors in our cars, mirrors in elevators, bathrooms, and entryways, magnified mirrors, mirrors on adjustable arms for revealing the back view, lighted mirrors, and, of course, full-length mirrors.

Your reflection is important to you, and what you reflect is critical to your success. But the glass mirror is a deceiver. The mirror offers a narrow one-dimensional view of your appearance. And it is an appearance that you have frequently rehearsed. It is that specific pose that you have grown to appreciate. You know the pose. It is often that last look before you leave ... head cocked, sly smile. Yet, how many times in a day will you be able to establish that stance and that pose so that others can view you as you have practiced and planned?

To present yourself well, you must consider that your reflection is much more complex than the glass mirror reveals. We need to practice more than the pose. You think what others see is not important? It is ... because you sell yourself—positive or negative—every minute, every day.

The most important, the most critical, the most telling reflection is not what you see. It is what others see. Granted, we all spend time in front of the mirror, but we spend vastly more time interacting with others. What do they see? They see more than a one-dimensional view. And it is that reflection which will impact your success.

Your face, body language, presence, and attitude are all constantly being watched and analyzed by those around you. Your voice, words, tone, and grammar are all being absorbed and compiled. Your emotions, demeanor, passion, your smile, and your eyes are all joining in to create the equation, the actual representation of how you are perceived. What are they seeing? Is it consistent with what you wanted them to see when you left that glass mirror? No one can see your intent, your heart, or the previous series of events that created your current demeanor. No one can see what you meant to convey.

You know that you have only one chance to make a first impression. But how long is that first chance? Five minutes? Thirty seconds? Think again. A series of experiments by Princeton psychologists Janine Willis and Alexander Todorov revealed that all it takes is a tenth of a second for people to form an impression of strangers from their face.[1]

A tenth of a second! Interestingly, longer exposures do not significantly alter those initial impressions.

Such a short encounter doesn't allow anyone to know your heart, motives, beliefs, goals, education, or intentions. In that short moment in time, you may not have enough warning to assume the special mirror pose. You are being examined by sight, smell, perceived mood, and overall physical appearance. You are being measured by posture, attitude, and expression. Quickly and often.

The good news is that you're in control of your reflection. But managing your true reflection is one of the most difficult things you'll ever do. It requires that you be willing to hear the little, inadvertent, unsolicited comments that people make — comments that are sometimes hurtful, flattering, surprising, or confusing but always worth consideration. Managing your reflection requires you to be willing to be honest with yourself and accept that others may be right. It requires you to admit that you may need to make some changes. Every comment, interaction, and response is worth internal analysis. Watch for input, wanted or unwanted, that offers a consistent message. And be willing to adjust your personal interface. What you thought you were communicating may not have been the message that you were actually conveying.

We love it when someone flatters us. Whether the pleasant comment was on hairstyle, clothing, actions, car—it doesn't matter. The point is that someone noticed we are or have something special. We eagerly accept that person's insight and wisdom.

But have you ever had someone walk up to you and make a comment like any of these:

"Are you feeling OK?"

"Smile! It's OK."

"Have you had a hard day?"

"You look tired."

"Is there something bothering you?"

You may have been surprised because you were feeling fine. If so, your appearance did not match your intent. You could consider the comments insulting and plan to volley some verbal retort that would precisely and strategically provide a perfect counterstrike, taking pleasure that you evened the score. That would be very gratifying. Or you could take the comments and place them in your internal database for analysis. Why, if you were feeling fine and energetic, were you sending a signal of the opposite? Not so much instant gratification.

The people you interact with are using their senses to analyze the overall consistency of the message you are sending. We often send conflicting messages unintentionally. Should you receive a negative, unfiltered comment about your appearance or countenance … stay cool. It does not mean you are a failure, that you are worthless, or that you have no future. It simply means you have been given an opportunity to better yourself. It means that you may not be presenting yourself the way you intended. You may need to smile more and talk less. You may need to listen more and joke less. You may need to be friendlier and complain less. You may need to take a firmer stance and be confident. You may need to try harder and stop making excuses. You are not compromising who you are. Rather, you are fine-tuning your overall personal representation.

Take control of your message, your presence, and your future. Accept any comments, even the negative ones, as assisting you to create a more powerful you. All comments can lead to a better you. A better you beats the competition.

Here's to you reflecting exactly what you want others to see and to you becoming Indispensable!

Take Action

How do you perceive yourself? Write down five characteristics that you believe describe you.

1.

2.

3.

4.

5.

Now, ask five people you work with to write down five characteristics that they believe describe you.

Are there gaps? Are you reflecting your intentions? Does the perception that others have of you match your appearance? Do comments from people you come in contact with match the characteristics that you believe describe you?

The Indispensable person is not ashamed of his or her reflection.

CHAPTER 5

Everything Counts

YOU CAN NEVER NOT LEAD. Everything you do, and everything you don't do, has an effect. You lead by acts of commission, and you lead by acts of omission. You are always leading and influencing.
—KENNETH AND LINDA SCHATZ

Ahhh, the galaxy of stars ... rock, pop, country, movie, TV, sports, and others in the great celestial realm. They tan. They pierce things. They tattoo up. They have "people." These appearance people style their hair, caulk on their makeup, stretch normal skin silly tight, install gleaming white teeth, and dress them in clothes not found on racks where you shop. The "stars" also have special coaches. These coaches teach them what to say and how to project an appropriate iconic image. Images that may be good ... wearing white hats and representing seemingly wholesome morals. Or images intentionally crafted to be bad ... a lone wolf, on the edge, dangerous, capable and willing to do anything, anytime to anyone. Most often, these publicly altered "imaged and handled" individuals are famous, rich, and deeply worried their fame may be fleeting. So they have business agents to keep them on the cover of magazines and gossip shows.

And you want to be like them. You may think that under that right set of circumstances and given the opportunity, you could be one of them.

Those "superstars" are illusions. They play a role. They act a part. They are selling. They have sold you, and you have bought. You are their fans. They say they "love you" during the award shows. They wink at you and blow you kisses. You watch and buy their posters, movies, and songs. You try to dress like them, tan like them, tattoo up like them, walk like them, and match their attitude.

But there are no cameras, no fans, and you don't have any "people." You're in a cubicle or behind a counter. What's the deal?

Consider your favorite rock star, movie queen, or TV tough guy on a day off camera. Do you think Mr. Jagger prances on a stage at home? Do you think Ms. Gaga is costumed up (or down) for breakfast? Do you think Mr. Eastwood stops real criminals carrying real guns with a tough-guy quote and a quick sucker punch? Nope. They have a day off, and they are not selling to you. Get it? Their images at work likely do not match their images away from their "work." But when the cameras are on, the image of what "their people" want you to see is displayed. They sell this image to investors, producers, talent scouts, tabloids, and you. It is what they do. It is their job. A great deal of money and resources are spent to build an image, set trends, and create their personal brand. And you fall for it. You are sold. Nothing you see is by accident. Their appearance, attitude, actions, and image are all planned, practiced, and presented.

Now, if it is indeed your hope and goal, you may one day "make it" into that celestial realm. When you do, someone will be there to assist you in creating your image, and your fans will model you. That is … when you make it. Today, now, in the interim, you have to create your image for those you encounter daily in what you do.

If you want to be successful in your job, you have to look successful for the job you have now. A safe way to portray success is to look and dress like those who are the most successful in your organization. Match your image to succeed at your current position. Should your star status change, you will have time to alter your style and appearance. Remember, everything counts: what you wear, how you act, your attitude, smile, hairstyle, hair color, facial hair, piercings, tattoos, overall tidiness, weight, height, eyewear, makeup, and how you use them all. Everything matters.

The harsh reality is that most organizations are often slow to embrace leading-edge culture. Perhaps it is because corporate leaders may not be a part of such modern culture practices. Perhaps it is because they seek to serve the interests of the majority of their potential customers. Perhaps it is because it is better to err on the side of caution. An organization may have a brand image it has created and has paid dearly to publicize, and it desires to protect it. It is likely an image the organization expects its employees to represent.

Careerbuilder.com reported a survey of 2,878 employers.[1] The goal was to find out if personal hygiene affected promotion decisions. What personal traits would keep an employee from advancing within the particular company? Here are the findings and percentages:

Piercings	37%
Bad breath	34%
Visible tattoos	31%
Wrinkled clothing	31%
Messy hair	29%
Dresses too casual	28%
Too much perfume or cologne	26%
Too much makeup	22%
Messy office	19%
Chewed fingernails	10%
Too sun-tanned	4%

Certainly there are exceptions. If you work at Zappos.com, it is completely different from working at IBM. The reality is that your appearance and actions are selling you—positive or negative. Is it fair? Perhaps not, but ...

Life is not fair.
—DAD

Organization leaders want people who reflect themselves positively and consistently to their customers. In like manner, you need to reflect positively to your "customers." Who are your "customers"? How about the managers where you are employed? How about the managers where you want to be employed? How about everyone who sees you and forms an opinion? You are always interviewing ... everything counts.

Although you may believe you have a right to be "you" at work, you are likely not protected by the First Amendment on the personal hygiene points previously listed. Sure you have the right to demonstrate your uniqueness however you desire, but the organization that employs you may also have the right to react to your statement of individuality. Successful organizations may have spent millions developing their brand and reputation. They will invest their resources to seek those who best represent their brand and message.

Let's suppose you have $100,000 to invest in the stock market. It is all the money you have, and you want the best advice, so you interview financial advisors. Let's say the three you interview all went to the exact same prestigious university, received the same grades, and graduated with the same degree:

> Advisor 1: Rock star hair, country star blue jeans, movie star tattoos, beer attitude

> Advisor 2: Tough-guy disposition, lone wolf, TV dude facial stubble, dark sunglasses

> Advisor 3: $1,000 suit, shined shoes, expensive watch, fancy pen

You have one minute to decide. You know nothing else about them. Whom do you choose?

You may be different from most people, but most would choose Advisor 3, who broadcasts a financial image.

Now, let's suppose that you plan to open a club on the trendy side of town. You want to project a cool image to attract young clientele who hang out late and spend money. You interview three people for the club manager opening:

Manager 1: Rock star hair, country star blue jeans, movie star tattoos, beer attitude

Manager 2: Tough-guy disposition, lone wolf, TV dude facial stubble, dark sunglasses

Manager 3: $1,000 suit, shined shoes, expensive watch, fancy pen

Whom would you choose? Your answer would be different from the first scenario.

What is your current employment position? With whom do you compete for better circumstances, position, and pay? How do successful people in your venue appear? Model them.

You are not competing with the personalities in the "great celestial realm." They compete with each other for public attention, adoration, and funding. Don't spend your energy attempting to look the part of those whom you never encounter. Don't give your adoration to people who would call the police if you knocked on their front door.

Too often hero status is given to people who do not warrant such reverence. Before you alter your appearance to match someone's persona and brand, stop and truly consider the results. Is it the image that allows you to compete with those around you? Before you make any permanent additions, alterations, and or statements with your physical appearance, understand that you may be compromising your opportunity to become Indispensable!

Model the successful people around you. Don't care? Not how you roll? That's your choice, but it is really good news for those who are competing against you for the next opportunity or promotion.

The bottom line is this: successful people understand that generally people like people like them. Get it? Read it again. People like people like them. More grammatically correct, people like people who share similar interests. This does not mean that successful people do not like diversity. On the contrary, successful people embrace diversity in people who protect their organizations' images. There is comfort, there is trust, and there is a bond. Find common ground, find similar interests, and seek rapport. Model the successful people in your business planning and opportunities. This does not distract from your individuality. Rather, it makes you accomplished. Playing a piano well does not make the musician a piano. Excelling at diagnosing auto engine problems does not make the mechanic a car. Understanding and interacting with people at their interest level will increase your skill set.

If you are absolutely sure that you want to have a certain visual edge that is unique and rather obvious, then look for businesses that cater to customers who are drawn to such a look. A company is likely to promote those who represent the company's brand rather than contradict it.

The goal of any organization is to achieve success. Promoting the organization's image is of value to it. Not promoting the organization's image is detrimental to its brand and its success. You may think that you are so far down the chain of command no one will notice or pay attention, but you would not be correct. The fact is that people are paying attention. Whether you are aware of it or not, everything you do counts. You are selling yourself, and indeed you will reinforce that you are exactly where you belong: trapped down at the bottom or indispensable and ready to move to the top.

DRESS LIKE YOU MEAN BUSINESS

> *Clothes make the man. Naked people have
> little or no influence on society.*
> —MARK TWAIN

If you want to *be* successful, you have to *look* successful. Two things that immediately influence other people are the expression on your face and the clothes you wear. Even if you don't think you have the money to spend on expensive clothes, buy the best you can afford. Think of the clothes you wear as an investment in your success.

In competitive situations, the candidate who looks healthy, happy, and energetic has a better chance of being promoted. You don't have to be an Adonis to win a promotion, but it is definitely to your advantage to take care of each aspect of your life—physical, emotional, spiritual, and intellectual—and apply a dab of shoe polish. Making sure that the shirt you plan to wear tomorrow is clean and pressed helps too. Take a look around. The people you admire and respect are usually those who look and act like people worthy of admiration and respect.

Looking successful is a choice. If you feel unattractive, have a makeover. If you want to wear a smaller size, exercise and lose the weight. If you want to feel more energized, take a brisk walk every morning before work. It's amazing how those endorphins you create with exercise will make you feel. Choose to do something for yourself.

There are plenty of books written about which clothes to wear, how to look taller, how to look thinner, or how to do just about anything you want to improve your appearance. You can easily research and learn what hairstyle, clothing strategy, eyeglass frames, shoes, and other accessories create your best appearance. Following the advice of books or stylists does not guarantee that you will look like a model on a magazine displayed at the grocery store. But unless your goal is to be a model on the front cover of a magazine at the grocery store, it does not matter. Your goal is to appear successful in your employment position. The appearance of success tells others you are successful and builds your own confidence.

Beware of fads, extremes, and clothes that are not right for business. Beware of clothes that strain or lose dominion over your skin. Beware of clothes you wore in high school, even if they still fit or if they once turned heads. If you find you are sharing clothes with any of your children, stop. There is the right time and place for your comfortable clothing, edgy attire, and your wild side ... but not when you need to be the Indispensable person for a promotion.

So, what about casual day? You know, that day when the company says wear those clothes you have been so anxious to show your fellow workers? Well, forget them. Change your perception to "less formal day." Casual day is a trap. The average person abuses casual day. The company envisioned one view when HR first suggested the day, but as time has progressed, the general workforce has pushed the original boundaries. Now the business population is showing up for work in holey jeans, T-shirts, and flip-flops. What a perfect situation for you! Certainly you can partake in casual day, but make sure your casual is more becoming than the general population. Always look better than what is expected. Not excessively better, not "in your face" better, not "holier than thou" better ... respectfully better.

A polished appearance communicates success, projects confidence, and encourages respect. Want to be treated casually? Dress casually. Look successful and polished, and you will gain confidence. People will notice your professional appearance. They will react to you differently.

Do you wear a uniform, smock, or some required attire? You still have an opportunity to look more successful than those around you. You control your neatness, attitude, actions, and ethics. You can stand out where you are. Many times people relax and succumb, displaying poor clothing habits in compliance with those around them rather than keeping a refined look. They apply for a position looking successful, but then they relax once hired. If appearance was important as a first impression, then it is important for all impressions thereafter. Why not continue to "apply" for greater opportunities by continuing to set an appearance example?

Take time to make sure your whole appearance is groomed well, whatever you are in control of ... hair, facial hair, body hair, eyebrows, teeth, nails, and so on. You notice and know when others are extreme in color, cut, style, or overall grooming. Just because it is on you does not change the real message sent.

Now shoulders back. Head high. Shoes shined. Workspace organized. E-mails answered. Give the appearance that you control your surroundings. Clothing better than expected, general grooming accomplished.

You are setting the standard. You are communicating that you aspire to more. You are becoming Indispensable!

Take Action

Study successful people in your profession. What choices have they made to help them reach their level of success? How do they act? Are they conservative? Are they formal? How do they dress? Find someone you admire in your actual field of work. Model that person's attitudes and style.

Determine what you can do to enhance your overall appearance. Check out some books on personal style and the best colors for your appearance. Phase out clothing that does not promote a professional image. Invest the time to project the appearance of a person whose life is under control, organized, and uncluttered.

Below are 10 Tips on Everything Counts:

1. Knowledge breeds confidence. Educate yourself on the rules of etiquette. Eliminate as many of etiquette's unknowns as possible.

2. One simple rule about office parties and business festivities: no matter what the occasion, it's still business, and moderation works best.

3. Don't eat at your desk. Eat food over a table, not the phone.

4. Save terms of endearment for those who are dear:

    "Honey" is something you spread on toast.

    A "Hun" is a warrior who followed Attila.

    A "deer" is an animal in the forest.

A "girl" is any female under age 12. A secretary or assistant is not a "girl."

None of those terms should be used in business.

5. To demonstrate character—don't be one.

6. Interrupting people's sentences is as rude as stepping on their toes.

7. Want to be the boss? Dress like one.

8. Speak on the phone the way you would speak to another person in the room. Use the same volume, and speak clearly and slowly enough for the other person to understand what you're saying. Never speak louder on your cell phone than you do on your landline. Speaking too loudly on your cell phone is tasteless and unnecessary.

9. Do not carry on a business conversation and read e-mails at the same time. When communicating, focus on one task at a time.

10. To learn what people are really like, ask three questions:

    What makes them laugh?

    What makes them angry?

    What makes them excited?[2]

Indispensable people have their act together.

CHAPTER 6

Unclutter, Unravel, and Transform

*Sometimes if you want to see a change for the better,
you have to take things into your own hands.*
—CLINT EASTWOOD

Quick! What do you think when you walk into a person's office that has piles of paper on the desk, an overflowing trash can, stale coffee on the table, and a generally sloppy appearance?

If you are like most, you probably walk away feeling that this person's life is out of control. You may wonder how he can ever get anything done. Where would he start?

Now, how do you feel when you walk into an office where the desk is relatively clean, things seem to be in order, and there is no sign of panic in sight?

Which of those two people do you think has the situation under control? Which person do you think would be indispensable to an organization or earn a promotion, assuming all other factors were equal? Sure, you would choose the neat freak—the orderly desk of the person who is obviously in control of his workspace, time, and appearance.

Unclutter

Fair or not, people make decisions on your organizational skills by what they see around your workspace. A cluttered desk is not a sign of being a busy, important person. The cluttered desk is a sign of confusion and indecision. It creates stress for most people. The Indispensable person is well organized and under control and transmits a confident appearance.

Uncluttering isn't confined to your desktop. Look at your calendar. Is it booked to the max, or do you have time to handle daily paperwork, routine tasks, and last-minute meetings? Do you have the time to complete the important things that pop up every day? Get yourself organized so that you will convey a sense of control, confidence, and pride that others would want to follow.

Here are 10 organizational tips that will help decrease the clutter:

1. Do you know where your time goes? Clutter is the result of not taking the time to clean up the mess. Keep track of how you spend your time for two weeks. OK, you may not want to do it for two weeks, but how about two days? The results will show you where your time is invested and where your time is "cluttered" up. Without tracking where your time is going, you will not know what to change. Once you understand the realities of where you are spending your time, you can begin to make decisions to improve.

2. Create a "to talk" or "e-mail draft" folder for your boss, subordinates, and peers. Unless it is a real emergency, wait until you have at least two items in the file before interrupting any of those people with your question. Better yet, send one e-mail a day with everything on that

e-mail from the day instead of sending numerous e-mails throughout the day. It will save you and the recipients time and frustration. You will also be surprised how many e-mails are not so important by the end of the day. Text messaging is the same. Do not text bomb every time something pops into your mind. Send texts only when immediate answers are required.

3. Take a speed-reading course. You could have read this book by now.

4. Close your door for 20 minutes, put up the do-not-disturb sign, and use that time to organize yourself every day.

5. Throw things away. Ask yourself, "What is the worst thing that could happen if I throw this away?" Most of the time, you can live with your answer, so start filling your wastebasket. What about electronic communications? Every computer has a delete button—make it your friend. Not comfortable throwing things away? Find the office "pack rat," and become his new best friend. Someone around the office has a copy of every memo and report from the past 10 years. Love that person—but throw your trash away.

6. Go to lunch at 11 a.m. or 1 p.m. to save both the time in the line and the time that it takes to get your food served. Going to lunch at noon will conservatively cost you at least 15 minutes a day … and the tip is the same. Think that is a good deal?

7. The key to paper and e-mail management is to keep it moving! Move the paper or e-mail to your out basket, your "to do" file, your "to read" folder, or your trash. Don't just let a message sit. Clean out your in basket!

8. Never clear off your desk by randomly throwing things in a drawer. You will eventually have to go through that drawer. Instead, create a logical system for storing these items in your desk.

9. If you only use a few lines of a report, ask the IT department for a reformat, if possible. Four pages when you need four lines just doesn't make sense—does it?

10. Do these four things before you leave the office: (1) Clear your desk. (2) Clear out your in basket and new messages. (3) Plan tomorrow's activities. (4) Enter your next day's to-do list in your organizer. Then go home. Planning the next day before you leave reduces stress and allows you to enjoy your time away from the office.

Everything counts! Sending a signal of being organized and under control will help separate you from everyone else as an Indispensable person.

UNRAVEL

Genius is the ability to reduce the
complicated to the simple.
—C.W. CERAM

Every year around the holidays, I find myself in a bad mood. Oh, don't get me wrong. I love the fun and festivities. But my mood is soured for a short period of time because of those darn lights we use to decorate our house.

At the end of each holiday season, I put them in the boxes so carefully. Yet when the next season rolls around, they have become one tangled mess. I spend several hours trying to unravel those dratted strings of lights. In the process I get frustrated, lose my holiday spirit, and get ready to go buy new lights. Last year's strings of lights have become my number one enemy.

Then, my wife comes along. She has a cool head. She takes the lights one strand at a time and unravels each strand without saying a word. Why is she able to fix the problem when I am frustrated and ready to start all over? I think the key difference is that she is patient, has a systematic way to unravel the lights, and understands the process.

Getting frustrated or angry or giving up will never help solve a problem at home or at work. The Indispensable person is a positive problem solver who follows a defined process.

One occupation that has to solve problems fast and effectively is that of airplane pilot. Think about how pilots approach a problem.

Let's suppose that a light begins flashing, signaling a hydraulic problem. The first thing the pilot does is check all of the instruments. Then, the pilot goes to the "black manual." The manual describes contingencies for almost every situation that could occur. The pilot then goes through the checkpoints, one by one, until the light quits blinking. The pilot knows then that the problem is solved.

Compare that with what happens in most organizations today. Maybe turnover is rampant, customers are going to competitors, or morale is low. Lights are flashing. What do we do?

Sometimes we throw a blanket over the flashing light so we can't see the annoying problem. We just ignore it and hope it will go away. However, most problems do not just disappear—rarely, if ever, will a problem disappear on its own.

The light is still flashing.

Some may want to change the bulb. Then, after replacing the bulb, the new bulb begins blinking just like the old bulb. Now, what can we do? How about smashing the bulb with a hammer? We may feel better because the bulb is no longer making that annoying flash, but we still have the same problem.

You see, most of the time, the bulb is not the problem. In reality, the issue is a systematic problem that has to be discovered and solved at the root. Same thing within work groups. Frequently, precious time is wasted finding someone to blame or passing the problem to someone else, instead of solving the problem that is making everyone look bad.

Every organization has plenty of people who can make situations worse. There is an abundance of those people. In contrast, the people striving to become indispensable are those who have unraveled the complexities of a situation, discovered the real facts, kept a cool head, followed a process, and solved the issue.

Notice that the pilot does not waste time figuring out who caused the problem. The pilot fixes the problem and then looks for the cause. Also, notice that my wife never blamed me for the tangled mess. She never took time to question each of the kids to see if any of them were at fault. I don't think that would have done much good anyway, do you? Instead, she chose to accept the wad of tangled wires and bulbs as it was and began unraveling the strands of lights.

Is unraveling a talent? You bet it is, and one key to unraveling is accepting total responsibility for the situation, regardless of the circumstances that got you to that point.

Most of the time, it is counterproductive to spend time finding someone to blame—and yes, there is always plenty of blame to go around. But, the Indispensable person is solution oriented and focuses on unraveling the problem and creating some viable alternatives. In winning organizations, the number one objective is to fix the problem, not fix the blame. And if you eliminate blame from your thoughts, you are on your way to becoming Indispensable!

Once you accept responsibility, you can move forward—into the solution mode.

The unraveling process is making molehills out of mountains. Most people look at a mountain as being too big or complex to attack. The Indispensable person looks at the mountain as a bunch of molehills put together that have to be unraveled—deconstructed one small piece at a time.

The unraveling process begins with clearly understanding the problem. What is the situation, the impact of the situation, and the desired result? Answer those three questions, and you are well on your way to getting the problem solved.

Next, what are the alternatives?

Are the alternatives doable, or do they cost too much in time, resources, and energy? You will know this step is complete when you understand the extent of the problem and know enough to solve all—or part—of it for good.

Then, develop a plan to execute. This is the easiest step of unraveling, if the other steps have been done properly. The Indispensable person is an unraveler who creates positive outcomes from negative situations.

TRANSFORM

> *The gem cannot be polished without friction, nor man*
> *perfected without trials.*
> —CHINESE PROVERB

Remember those cool little robots that could be changed into intergalactic fighting machines when you were a kid? They changed from humanoid robots to awesome war machines, but you had to know what buttons to push to make the transition occur.

So, what does this have to do with becoming indispensable?

The Indispensable person is probably going to be someone who knows what buttons to push, someone who is a transformer—a change agent. Isn't it interesting how people are so adverse to change ... almost any kind of change? Even changes that are obviously for the good are met with resistance.

"The only constant is change" has been a universal truth since it was reportedly first stated in 500 BC. Why, then, are most people so uncomfortable with change? It is probably because change requires leaving their comfort zone and moving into the unknown. Without change, though, people have a tendency to get into a rut of doing the same things the same ways. Should we be surprised when we get the same results?

Remember this: eventually, a rut can become a grave because the only difference between a rut and a grave is the depth. When you are in a rut, the first thing you need to do is to quit digging. Experience tells us that we cannot improve without making some kind of change. In fact, preparing to be indispensable will require change. So the question is not if change will happen, but rather, how are you going to transform the change to a positive event?

I heard about an experiment several years ago to evaluate reaction to change. Four tubes were laid side by side on the floor. A cube of cheese was placed in the second tube. A mouse was then released, and it immediately went to the first tube. Finding the tube empty, the mouse proceeded to the second tube. There it discovered and ate the cheese, which met its basic need for survival. The mouse then returned to its point of release.

The next day, the mouse followed the same routine by going to the empty first tube, eating cheese from the second tube, and returning to its point of release. The mouse repeated the same routine for several days. Finally, realizing that it was a waste of time going to the first tube, the mouse began going directly to the second tube. The mouse ate the cheese, met its need for survival, and went back to its point of release. This routine also continued for several days.

The people conducting the experiment moved the cheese to the third tube the next day. The mouse went directly to the second tube, where its needs had always been met, and there was no cheese.

What was the mouse's response? Did it go back to the first tube looking for the cheese? No. Did it go back to where it had started? No. Did it go to the third tube searching for the cheese? No.

The mouse chose to stay in the second tube where its need for survival had always been met and waited for the cheese to come to it. If allowed, the mouse would have starved in the second tube, waiting for the cheese—instead of reacting to the change.

Doesn't this sound familiar? "Let's wait," they say. "We have always done it this way, and it has always worked in the past!"

So, what's the point? There are a couple.

First, when things change, you need to make sure you don't "starve to death" waiting for things to go back to the way they used to be. Doing things the way you always have, being warm and fuzzy in your comfort zones, can be the greatest enemy to your potential.

Second, the best time to make change is when things are going well, rather than when you have a problem in sight. If the mouse had been searching for more cheese while it was meeting its basic need of survival, it might have discovered a whole block of cheese in the third tube.

Therein lies the paradox of change: the best time to change is when it seems the least necessary. Why? Because you are able to move forward with a clear mind rather than being distracted by your current issues.

You can transform yourself by being enthusiastic about yourself and your work. Enthusiasm is as important to your success as how you dress, how you look, how much skill you have, how much education you've accumulated, and how gifted you think you are.

The good news is that you have an opportunity to choose the attitude you will have for each situation every day. You have control over how you respond to your situation. Whether it is a change in job assignments, the way you spend your lunch hour, or your attitude while you're in your car driving to work—you have control.

All too often people want to blame their attitude about something on past events and experiences in their lives. Charles Dickens once advised, "Reflect upon your present blessings, of which every man has many—not on your past misfortunes, of which all men have some." Don't brood over mistakes, carry grudges, or harbor hate. Each of those negative emotions possesses the power to prevent you from accomplishing the success you desire.

The Indispensable people are transformers! They make change a positive experience for everyone around them.

Take Action

Three of the common criteria that are evaluated in job interviews are these:

1. Is this candidate organized enough to handle additional responsibilities?

2. Can this candidate solve problems?

3. How well does this candidate handle change?

You can separate yourself from your competition right now by being a champion in all three of those areas.

If you are like most, the most challenging of the three is solving problems. Problems will not solve themselves and just disappear. The good news is that you can become a champion problem solver by following a systematic process.

Here Is a Path to Follow

Problem solving begins with a clear understanding of what caused the problem—not just the results of the problem. The best way to understand is to write the problem on paper. Writing clarifies the situation. If you are serious about solving a problem, you will need to write each of the following on paper:

1. Clearly state the problem.

2. Describe the impact of the problem.

3. Describe what you want to happen: what will be the result of solving the problem?

4. List at least three alternatives for solving the problem.

5. Pick the best alternative and create a plan.

6. Implement the plan.

The Indispensable person is a positive problem solver and change transformer.

A small trouble is like a pebble. Hold it close to your eye, and it fills the whole world and puts everything out of focus. Hold it at a proper distance, and it can be examined and properly classified. Throw it at your feet, and it can be seen in its true setting, just one more tiny bump on the pathway of life.
—CELIA LUCE

*It is the positive connections with those around us
that make life worth living.*
—DAVID COTTRELL

CHAPTER 7

Shh ... Listen

The art of conversation lies in listening.
—MALCOLM FORBES

A friend was going to a party where he would be meeting his wife's coworkers from her new job for the first time. He felt anxious as the time for the party grew near, and he wondered whether they would like him or not. He rehearsed various scenarios in his mind in which he tried in different ways to impress them. He grew more and more tense.

But on the way to the party, the man came up with a radically different approach, one that caused all of his anxiety to melt completely away.

He decided that, instead of trying to impress anyone, he would spend the evening simply listening to them and summarizing what they had just said. At the party, he spent the evening listening carefully to everyone, responding with phrases like, "I understand what you're saying; you feel strongly that ..." and "Let me see if I understand what you mean ..." He also avoided voicing his own opinions, even though at times it meant biting his tongue to keep from doing so.

To his amazement, he discovered that no one noticed or remarked on the fact that he was just listening. Each person he talked to during the evening seemed content to be listened to without interruption. On the way home, his wife (whom he had not told about the experiment) told him that a number of people had made a point of telling her what a remarkable person he was. The word "charismatic" was used by one person to describe him, while another said he was one of the most "articulate" people she had ever met.[1]

Could it be that charisma and brilliance have as much to do with how we listen as what we say? Imagine a world in which people actually listened to one another, rather than just waiting for the other people to stop talking so they can give their opinion.

Do you want to influence people? Do you want to fascinate them and gain their admiration? Do you want to delight them in compelling conversation?

Then listen. Ask questions and listen. **Don't be afraid of silence.** Silence is loud. It allows you the time to think and articulate your thoughts more effectively.

Everyone has stories, opinions, and beliefs. Everyone has passions. It is likely that people are more emotionally fascinated with their own experiences than yours.

So ask, listen, pay attention, ask a follow-up question, and remember the details of the interaction. Stop and engage. By taking the time to ask, you express your engagement and curiosity.

You will delight the person who is talking. Your bonus is that you will probably learn something as well.

We are often too eager to tell, relate, instruct, offer opinions, and give our life story. But stop. When you ask others to share and you attentively listen to their thoughts, you make them feel that they are important and of consequence to you. When you ask questions, it affirms that you are actually hearing them. When you remember the subject matter and recall it at a later date, it increases their esteem for you. Smile, nod your head, agree, laugh, and participate in their accounts. Making those around you feel important elevates your reputation and position. People want to know you care.

Becoming a great listener will help you become indispensable and separate you from your competition for the next opportunity. In most cases, we should spend about 75 percent of our time listening, 10 percent of our time thinking about what we've heard, and 15 percent of our time talking. If you're talking 50 percent of the time in a conversation, you're talking too much and not listening enough.

One of the deepest needs of all people is to be heard and understood. Miscommunication occurs largely because we do not take the time to listen. Slow down, and don't assume you know what is going to be said before they say it. Alexander Pope once said, "Some people never learn anything because they understand everything too soon."

Listening effectively is not easy. It requires three things that most people lack: time, patience, and concentration. Yet other people judge how much you care about them by how attentive you are to what they are saying. If you listen to hear only what you want to hear, you lose credibility as well as trust. To become indispensable, you have to make connections with people. Connecting begins with listening.

How do you feel when someone interrupts you? Annoyed? Frustrated? Disrespected?

Interrupting is the greatest distraction to anyone talking because it signals that something, someone, some thought, or you consider yourself more important and relevant than the person speaking. Whether you are part of a crowd or one-on-one with the person speaking, respect that person's narrative and her dignity. Allow the person the freedom to complete her thought or story. Any disturbance you initiate communicates selfishly and negatively to the speaker. Give the speaker the courtesy of your undivided attention. Should you have time issues or need to delay the discussion in process, then do so graciously. If the discussion is one-on-one, then tell the speaker you have a time constraint but you do want to continue the discussion later. And offer the speaker a reason to believe you found the interaction engaging. It is possible that the subject matter may never be rekindled or thoughts completed. But it is valuable to protect another person's dignity.

People never forget how you make them feel. When someone feels slighted or insignificant, you lose that person's respect, and it is hard to get it back.

Here are some listening pointers to utilize:

- Stop what you are doing and focus on the speaker.

- Smile. Demonstrate that you want to be there and you are happy to listen.

- Maintain eye contact.

- Think about what the speaker is saying, not on something that might be on your mind.

- Don't interrupt or complete the speaker's sentence.

- Acknowledge that you are listening with appropriate facial expressions.

- Ask questions in follow-up: "Tell me more about ..." or "Why ... ?"

- As the discussion concludes, offer a positive comment about the conversation.

- Do your best to remember key thoughts for later follow-up.

Remember that the speaker may not be seeking your input or your experience. If you are confident that the speaker truly desires your input during a discussion, then offer your views. But keep in mind that often the speaker may simply need someone to truly listen to her thoughts. The speaker will be delighted to have your complete attention and fascination.

Yes, you have stories and opinions too. There will be times when you can tell them. There will be many opportunities for you to interact and share. There may be times when you desire undivided attention from someone. But you will find a new level of trust with people when you truly listen to them. As a product of that trust, they will listen to you as you have listened to them.

Keep the natural ratio of ears and mouth—2 to 1—intact in your communications. It may be tough because we have the ability to speak about 120 to 150 words per minute while we are able to process about 500 words per minute. That makes it doubly tough to be a great listener. But the Indispensable person is not the average person. Separate yourself by listening with patience, respect, and focus.

Take Action

Here are some specific skills to practice that will help you become a better listener:

- Focus on looking squarely in one eye of the speaker. Yes, one eye. This little trick subconsciously blocks out distractions and gives the speaker your total attention. Try it.

- Don't just sit there. Interact. And if you lose the context of the subject, ask for clarification. Be open. Make sure that your shoulders are square with the person you are listening to, and try not to cross your arms.

- Ask questions. Questions show that you care.

- Recap. Sum up the main points as you go along, such as, "So, you think we can get to Point B more easily by setting up a rest stop between Points A and B?"

- Don't finish the speaker's thoughts, even though you may get her point.

- Don't interrupt unless the building is on fire.

- Nod your head—not as though you are at a concert but in a way that reassures the speaker that you are taking in information.

The Indispensable person respects those around him by being a terrific listener.

CHAPTER 8

Speech Matters

Um, like, well, uh, you know, so,
I guess this is chapter ...

Your very first word was likely greeted with great celebration and pride. Parents shared the single-syllable word with grandparents, friends, and very distant relatives. They danced, you danced, and everyone ate ice cream. You spoke your word again, and laughter accompanied by jubilant applause brought the house down. You hadn't caused such celebration since the day you first rolled over. As time progressed, you learned even more words. You also learned how to color those words with emotion. Whining, tears, cutesy smiles, big eyes, and all-out, fall-on-the-ground tantrums were some of the passionate enhancements you added to the spoken words. You learned that your words would generate rewards and reactions. By the age of five, you had become a master communicator, capable of changing the plans and mood of your parents at a moment's notice.

Then the bell rang, and the rules set in. Verb tenses, synonyms, homonyms, sentence structures, preposition issues, *i* before *e* except ...

Regional and family dialects and accents were incorporated into your verbal patterns. Some neighborhood slang and attitude were added apparently to confuse many. Maybe you learned to talk fast—or slow with strange inflections—or to be quiet and say little. Somewhere along the way you may have taken to mumbling, stuttering, or talking too low. Maybe you sounded like the voice coming from a drive-through speaker.

Whatever the case, it has gone downhill since that very first word. It went from party time to panic time if you had to speak in front of a group of people.

Now you are an adult. You are in the business arena. The phone rings. You recognize your boss's voice on the other end of the line.

> Congratulations. Your team did it again! For the past several months, your department's performance has consistently set the pace for our company. You're doing a great job! I want to recognize your team's performance at our next senior management meeting, and I have arranged to put you on the agenda for a 20-minute presentation. We want you to share with the rest of the company the great things your team has been doing. Our entire senior staff is looking forward to hearing what you have to say.

After talking a few more minutes, you hang up the phone.

"Wow," you say to yourself, "this is a great opportunity to provide recognition for my team ... and to receive some well-deserved recognition for myself. Upper management actually wants to take the time to listen to what I have to say. This is great!"

Then reality sets in … and you begin thinking about the task.

"Wait a minute," you say. "I have to deliver a 20-minute presentation in front of people I don't know? I know my stuff, but what if I fail? This could be career suicide. Why did I agree to do this?"

From great honor to career suicide in 30 seconds. How could one assignment send anyone on that type of an emotional trip? Easy. The task is making a presentation … one of mankind's greatest fears. Do you think that speaking in public became the number one fear by accident? No way. That status was earned. But there are things that you can do to attack that fear.

Why is something as natural as talking often a stressful, dreaded experience when you have to speak in front of an audience? Studies have shown that people fear public speaking more than snakes, heights, sickness, and even death. Jerry Seinfeld once quoted those statistics and said if this is the case, "You would be better off in the coffin than delivering the eulogy"—a pretty harsh penalty for not wanting to speak in public.

A fear that is greater than the fear of death itself? This is great news! This is to be celebrated. You should dance and laugh. This can be a game changer! Becoming a great speaker will help you become Indispensable!

Speaking to groups—of two or three or even a roomful—is required for advancement in almost any industry. As an executive, you will often be asked to "say a few words" about your product, department, or even yourself. The good news is that public speaking is a skill that can be developed.

So how do you get started? One of the best ways to improve speaking skills is to teach others what you know. You are completely comfortable with the subject and can speak about it with ease. You will find that teaching others what you know will teach you how to communicate more effectively.

Some people may have to jump off the deep end and start speaking in public to get beyond the fear of speaking. You may not be ready for a large audience right off the bat, but the basic activities of speaking are the same, regardless of the size of the audience. So go ahead and take the first step to start gaining confidence. Begin to develop your own personal style. You can volunteer to represent your organization at public functions, speak at civic clubs, participate in services at your church or synagogue, teach a class, or make a presentation at work.

Each time you speak in front of a group, you will become more comfortable and your influence will become stronger. That is if you reduce unnecessary words, deploy proper verb tenses, polish your sound, work on correct pronunciation, and deliver with confidence.

OK, so it may not be easy, but if it were easy, it would not be a game changer. With effort, practice, and a little attention to detail, you can change your verbal communication skills and literally awe those who remain locked in fear. The smartest thoughts, the most creative ideas, and the best strategies are wasted if they cannot be communicated well. The perfect suit, dress, shoes, tie, and haircut will be devalued if you cannot speak appropriately. It is critically important to your success. And you are in control of it.

Golfers, musicians, the military, firefighters, pilots, and people in a million other businesses and professions spend time practicing their trade. Then they practice more. Practice readies them for the real thing and creates positive habits. Changing your communication abilities requires practice—dedicated and focused practice.

So how can you practice your speaking so that you can become indispensable? Try these five steps.

STEP 1. LISTEN TO YOURSELF

Hearing yourself has never been easier. Smartphones, recorders, PCs, and even our cars can now record our own voices and conversations. Record yourself in an informal dialogue between friends. Record yourself reading an article from the newspaper. Record yourself having a telephone conversation. Record yourself talking to the dog.

Now listen to the recordings. Listen as others hear you. But, you say, "I would rather not because I don't like the way I sound." Bingo! That is the point.

Compare the sound of your voice to that of your local news anchor, sportscaster, or radio host. Identify the things you need to improve. Record yourself over and over. Try different tones, inflections, sentence rhythms, and speeds. Like playing a musical instrument, it will take time. Keep recording and listening.

Try some readings to sound friendly. Try some to sound energetic. Try some to sound interested. People will react differently to you if you sound involved and excited to speak with them. Smile as you speak. Stand while you speak. What if you answered every call enthusiastically, making the caller feel welcome, rather than without emotion? It will make a difference in how your conversation goes. Listen to yourself, and practice developing an enthusiastic tone when talking to others.

It's not what you say. It's how you say it.
—Mom

Step 2. Delete Brainless Words

Um, well, like, uh, you know, man—you see what I mean?

There are many words and phrases we habitually say that mean nothing. Sometimes we say them to get a sentence rolling. Sometimes we say them because we don't know what to say. Sometimes they are simply verbal habits. Whenever we say them, they are likely a waste of breath and a shining beacon to all who hear us that we are verbally challenged.

It is probable that these words are simply word behaviors or crutches that you developed over time. If so, identify and know what your brainless utterances are. Once you become aware of them, eliminate your dependency on them. Make mental notes and corrections each time you say them. Ask someone you know to tap you each time you say one. Get a jar and put a dime in it for every verbal slip-up. Within a few weeks, your diligence and self-correction will reduce your repetitive use of brainless and meaningless jargon.

These words may also be part of your response pattern. You may be subconsciously using them to gain your thoughts and plan your response. If so, there are better methods. For instance, if someone asks you a question that takes a moment to grasp or assemble a response, you might try repeating the question. This does two things: first, it suggests you were indeed listening to the speaker intently, and second, it provides you that moment to think about the response. Another nonverbal pause you could deploy is the "contemplation look"—you know the one, looking up at the ceiling, a little pain showing on your face as if you are really considering the appropriate answer. Both of these examples are not to become habits either, or we will have to add another chapter to this book on how to stop habitual contemplation looks. The truth is that the electronics in your brain are much faster than the mechanics in your mouth. You can lessen the dependence on those brainless verbal utterances. Yes you can! Practice.

Another set of phrases that should be eliminated are associated with the word *honest*. You may be using these phrases unintentionally and without underlying meaning, but inadvertently you are giving the listener some concern. Do you say these phrases?

"To be honest with you …"

"Honestly …"

"I can honestly say …"

"In all honesty …"

In most cases, you are simply buying time with these sentence intros. Or perhaps you do want to communicate that most often you cannot be trusted, unless you announce your intention to be honest … this time. Better to always be trusted than only when you announce and proclaim it—honestly.

Finally, lose the off-color words in any business setting. You may have to deploy the same methods used to eliminate brainless utterances. Just because you are comfortable with using off-color words does not mean your listeners are. Using these words is most likely a habit, and they can be replaced with more accurate and informative adjectives.

STEP 3. GRAMMAR TIME

Forget about the fact that you did not like grammar in school. You have been around long enough to recognize when those around you are using improper grammar. You may have said something and then felt that it did not sound correct. You may not use the proper verb tense. You may end your sentences with a preposition too often. You know what your tendencies are. Pay attention to the details of your speech because other people are. Listen to yourself, and make mental notes of grammatical errors. You have great ideas. Do not let them be clouded and inaccurately judged because of poor grammar. Care about your grammar, spoken and written.

Get a book, look it up online, or use the spelling and grammar checker on your computer. Here are some examples of grammar points you need to know:

- Understand when to use *I, me*, or *myself; she* or *her; he* or *him; we* or *us*; and *they* or *them*.

- *Hisself* is not a word.

- *Irregardless* is not a word.

- Get a grasp on *who* and *whom*.

- Need I go *further* or *farther*?

STEP 4. LEARN SOME NEW WORDS

You don't have to study the dictionary. You don't have to be a walking thesaurus. You don't need to become all scholarly. Learn 10 or 20 new words a year, and use them. You will surprise those around you, and you'll increase your communication skills.

Try these:

> *Algorithm:* a method for solving a mathematical problem
>
> *Anomaly:* an unexpected result that deviates from the standard
>
> *Cavalier:* given to offhand dismissal of important matters
>
> *Exacerbate:* to increase the irritation or annoyance of something
>
> *Salient:* standing out conspicuously, prominently

Additionally, there are words that you already know that offer emotion. Some words add color and personality to your communication. They seem to paint a picture.

Try these and think of your own:

Valiant	Gorgeous	Fascinated
Captivating	Magical	Enthralled
Compelled	Mystery	Gracious
Magnetic	Zealous	Serene

STEP 5. STAND INTO THE SPOTLIGHT

Now, if most people are deathly frightened to speak in front of others, then you have an incredible opportunity to stand apart. It may take courage, but the more you practice, the better prepared you will be. You have been working on your tone, reducing the brainless words, using correct grammar, smoothing your dialect, and increasing your vocabulary. Time to put it all together.

You may have an opportunity at work, church, school, civic organization, or at a celebration. Use the moment to give a prepared speech and show all the cowards how to do it the right way.

A basic speech, and one that will work for you time and time again, is simple to construct. It usually has three parts:

- An introduction

- The speech body, which is generally taught to be three points

- The conclusion

The introduction is important. Should you need to exchange some pleasantries or address the welcome you received, then do so. But once the speech starts, then go for the introduction. The goal is to gain the listeners' attention. You want them to be interested in what you are about to say. You want to offer insight about your topic. You could ask a question that may intrigue them. You could use humor. You could startle them with a statistic they did not know. The introduction should prepare them for the subject you are about to cover. But never, never, ever begin your speech with statements like these:

"I'm very nervous." (even if you're shaking)

"I did not have time to prepare." (even if you didn't)

"My name is …" (sort of boring, and everyone else does it already)

"I'm not good at speaking." (even if you are not)

"Well, uh, like …" (Did you read the beginning of this chapter?)

If you do not believe in yourself, your abilities, or your knowledge, then your listeners will not waste their time believing in you either. A good introduction alerts the listeners that something interesting, different, creative, informative, and important is about to happen.

Their brains suddenly acknowledge that you are different. You will have their attention.

> *Bad example:* "I have been asked to speak to you about heart disease."

> *Call-to-attention example:* "Did you know heart disease is the single leading cause of death in the United States?"

The subject is the same, but the listeners will respond differently.

The speech body is important. Cover your points thoroughly, but do not repeat words, sentences, thoughts, or subjects. Know what you're talking about … be an expert. Be confident, smile, and use eye contact, hand motions, passion, and inflection. If it is a somewhat formal speech, you can have notes to help you through your subject matter. But never read your speech to your listeners! Notes are to prompt you and keep you on track. And when your subject and your points are through, you are through. Go to your conclusion. Rambling will cause you to lose your momentum and your listeners.

The conclusion is important. In summary format (short), tell your listeners what you told them in the body. Draw the conclusion for them. Give them a final short statement to prove, convince, remind, and persuade them that the subject of your speech was compelling and worthy of action. But never end with statements like these:

> "I guess that is about it."

> "That's all I have."

> "I'm glad that's over."

> "I hope that made sense to you."

If you cannot draw a conclusion to what your speech was about, your listeners probably couldn't either. If you did not challenge, educate, persuade, or convince your listeners, then you learned that you have areas to improve.

You may never be completely comfortable speaking in front of an audience. You may always be nervous. You may never like it. But public speaking will separate you from your competition, and you can get there.

Now it is time to practice. Create a speech that introduces you or is about your favorite food, your job, or your favorite movie. Give the speech to yourself in front of the mirror. Give it to your dog. Give it to your cell phone while recording it. Take a course in speech at a community college, or join an ongoing education group on public speaking. Find a Toastmasters group, or start one at your company.

Remember, the majority of our communication is nonverbal. Our facial expressions, appearance, hand motions, and voice tone add definition and confirmation to what we say. Listeners are constantly scanning us to see if there are any contradictions in our message. Facial expressions and body language that do not match the subject matter will result in disbelief, and you will lose your audience.

You may not have to do it often, but if you can compose yourself and deliver an enjoyable, informative speech, whether to one person or a thousand, you will differentiate yourself from others. Remember, almost everyone is afraid of public speaking. You have the opportunity to demonstrate to them that you are more brave and capable. You have conquered a fear that constricts their talents. You have separated yourself. People will notice and listen. You will become Indispensable!

Take Action

The best way to improve your public speaking skills is to do public speaking. It may start with speeches to your mirror or your pet. But eventually you will need to try it on others. Public speaking does not always mean you have to prepare a speech. It could be in the form of better communication to customers and coworkers.

If there are organizations within your company, community, or church that would allow you to practice public speaking, join them, volunteer for them, and participate. Although it will take you out of your comfort zone, it will prepare you to for that time when you need to shine.

Here are 10 great tips[1] to remember to help you wow your audience:

1. **A comforting thought is to know that most people in the audience want you to do well.** They are on your side. Have you ever gone to a presentation, hoping to see the presenters fall on their faces? Of course not. Your audience wants you to be successful, which is why they are investing their time to hear what you have to say.

2. **Be yourself.** Your presentation is not about being perfect. It is about "connecting with others" and delivering a sincere message. Audiences want to hear from people who are genuine.

3. **Proper preparation and rehearsal can reduce nervousness by 75 percent.** Proper breathing techniques can reduce nervousness by another 15 percent. Your mental state accounts for the remaining 10 percent.

4. **State your three major points in a positive, proactive manner.** People are often defensive when problems are presented, while audiences are generally more enthusiastic when they hear about opportunities. Examples: "We can improve customer satisfaction" instead of "We are losing customers." "We can increase profits" instead of "We are losing money." "We can retain our valuable employees" instead of "We are losing our best employees."

5. **Almost memorize the beginning of your presentation.** Nervousness is most intense at the beginning of a presentation. Attack your nerves by having your introduction totally under control.

6. **Practice looking confident.** Many people judge confidence by your posture, body language, and voice tone. The more you practice looking confident by practicing in front of a mirror, spouse, or coworker, the more confidence your audience will see when you stand in front of them.

7. **Talk to yourself the way your best friend would talk to you.** If your best friend were with you, he or she would be building your confidence by telling you that you will do great, that you are prepared, and that you are going to have fun. Chances are your friend is probably right, so talk to yourself on your friend's behalf. (No one will ever know.)

8. **When you step in front of the room, your smile should confidently suggest, "I'm glad to be here."** If you let your audience know you are happy to be there, the group will probably be happy to have you there as well.

9. **The Presenter's Creed is this:**

   (1) Tell them what you are going to tell them,

   (2) tell them, and

   (3) tell them what you told them.

10. **What your audience loves and hates:**

Loves	**Hates**
Enthusiasm	Lectures
Entertainment	Boasting
Expertise	Arrogance
Confidence	Long-windedness
Conversation	Insults

Becoming a great speaker can be your ticket to becoming indispensable. Practice your presentation so much that you can do it "on autopilot." That way, even if your brain freezes, your lips can keep moving.

CHAPTER 9

Write Can Be Wrong

It was the best of communications. It was the worst of communications. It was the age of the ability of e-mail. It was the age of the inability of e-mail.

There have been incredibly gifted writers like Charles Dickens, Shakespeare, and Edgar Allen Poe. They had the ability to color and animate their words, allowing us to feel their inner thoughts and emotions. They were artists who could transport us with ink on paper, causing us to dream, causing us to love, and causing us to read stuff in school.

Then there is a new, different language of e-mail, texting, instant messaging, and assorted social media networks.

You do not have to write like Dickens, Shakespeare, or Poe. But if you are going to become indispensable, you will have to write effectively. Your written words must reflect your message accurately.

The key to effective writing is being clear and concise. People become choked on unnecessary words on paper. Think about it. The Lord's Prayer is 66 words, the Gettysburg Address consists of

286 words, and the Declaration of Independence has 1,332 words. Yet the U.S. government regulations on the sale of cabbage totals 26,911—about as many words as are in the book you are reading. Does that make sense?

A general rule is that people comprehend and understand sentences of 15 words or less. When writing, 12 words per sentence will do in most cases. A paragraph should consist of eight or fewer sentences.

Whatever you write, your objective is clarity. Clarity begins with simplification. If you want to connect through memos, reports, and other written communication, start simplifying everything now.

For practice, pull four recent memos from your file. It does not matter whether you received or sent the memo. Count the words on the page. Now rewrite the memo, but use only half the words. If you are like most, you will be able to make your point with more clarity by eliminating unnecessary words.

Those who receive memos, reports, and other documents have limited time to read and comprehend your ideas. Write to save the reader time. If a word isn't relevant, leave it out. If the reader can comprehend the idea without multiple details, delay them until later. Get the reader's buy-in. Then add the less important details.

Today much of our communication is instant and spontaneously transmitted—sometimes to a location a few inches away. We communicate without the benefit of facial expressions (☺ does not count), audible tones, or hand gestures. This increases the challenge in communicating effectively.

Business e-mail (and text messages) can be misunderstood easily. No one can read facial expressions and body language electronically. What you happily keyed—may be read angrily. What you keyed innocently—may be read as contempt. What you keyed humorously—may be read as offensive. You think you have written a masterpiece, but the reader may find it confusing and never finish it. You may never know what you really communicated. You may have touched a nerve, started a feud, or created an adversary innocently and unintentionally.

If such misunderstanding is easily achieved with simple written messages, then the possibility of communication failure with more sensitive matters is high. Be careful.

Never respond in writing to anyone if you are responding in anger. Stop, and cool down first. If you do not completely understand an event, message, or request, get clarification before you reply. If you have received an e-mail and it has stirred your emotions, remember, you may not have understood the writer's intent. You have no confirmation of facial expression.

Be careful with any of your responses that seem to correct or "call out" the recipient. For instance, avoid phrases and statements like these:

"I have already sent that to you." (and then forward the e-mail you sent a week ago)

"I told you …"

"I said to …"

"Stop DOING that!" (Don't type action words in all CAPITALS.)

"Did you not see my e-mail yesterday?"

"Everybody knows that."

"You were wrong."

Instead of calling out the recipient, you can deflect and diffuse the emotion in a situation by allowing the person an out with dignity:

"It may have gotten hung up in the e-mail server."

"Did I mention ... ?"

"I know you already know this, but I ..."

"Could you help me with ... ?"

"Share with me your thoughts on ..."

Disarm and diffuse. Gain cooperation, not grudges. Disarming and diffusing the emotional content of situations may not give you the opportunity and enjoyment of proving you were right. You may not have a chance to set the record straight or get even. But you may get a chance to gain an ally. No one appreciates a response he or she considers belittling or disrespectful. If you have any question about the way your message may be received, ask someone else to read it before you hit Send.

Perhaps you admire some billionaires who speak their mind and say it like it is. These people are on TV, able to say whatever they want to whomever they want. You can do that too ... once you are a billionaire and have TV shows who want to interview you. Until then, you may have much better success building rapport than building your ego.

If you supervise or manage workers who need correction, you must do so. But remember, you may well create more issues with any communication that does not allow the recipient the opportunity to observe and confirm your intent and expression.

E-mail is not only a poor communication vehicle for definitive interactions but it also has traps. How about those Reply, Reply All, and Forward functions? More eyes, more alternate viewpoints, more opportunities to be misunderstood, and a bigger quagmire. The point is, there are no simple e-mails. Never write anything in an e-mail that communicates a subject, words, or a tone that you consider private. There are no private e-mails—they have a way of creating a life of their own.

There is rarely an appropriate time to forward an internal e-mail to an external reader. Somewhere within that e-mail string there may be some verbiage that could embarrass, alarm, or irritate an outside reader, not to mention people within your organization. Keep your internal e-mails internal.

Remember, everything counts. There is really no need to use special exotic fonts, colored fonts, e-mail wallpapers, pictures of your dog, and graphics like smiley faces with your e-mail. Remember, everything communicates. Your favorite color, font, wallpaper, dog, or graphic may communicate something different to the recipients. It may not be their favorite color, or perhaps they were once bitten by a dog just like yours. You never know. You have nothing to gain by sending personal graphics. In fact, doing so may even send a message that will prevent you from becoming indispensable.

An e-mail is virtually permanent, irreversible, and can be shared with others. You have no control over where it goes after you hit Send. Furthermore, deleted messages can later be resurrected. Use discretion and caution. Confidential e-mail messages do not exist.

Any communication you send represents you. You will likely never know if further explanation was needed or if it was received as you intended.

If you want to become indispensable, protect your reputation and message with every written communication.

Take Action

When you hit the Send button, you lose control over how your message may be accepted. Here are a few things to do before you hit Send:

1. If it is an important message, print and read it before sending. If it is really important, print, read, hold until the next day, read again, and then hit Send. You can't take it back once you hit Send.

2. Never forward jokes, political rants, or pictures to business associates. They receive enough from people who are not trying to become indispensable.

3. Use Reply All rarely. Make sure that "all" need to know before you waste their time.

4. Never send anything in e-mail that you wouldn't want the world to read. E-mails have a way of mysteriously appearing in weird places.

5. Use e-mail as a tool. Don't overuse e-mail. When people receive a message from you, they should know it is important.

From this point forward, be conscious and in control of every written communication you send or post. Be aware that the message may be seen by people you never intended to see it. It may be posted on a random site. It may suggest multiple meanings. Write it as though you would not be ashamed if everyone in the world read it.

The Indispensable person does not try to impress with big words, long sentences, or verbose statements. The Indispensable person communicates clearly, concisely, and to the point.

SECTION FOUR

Business Rules

*To be successful, you have to have your heart in your
business, and your business in your heart.*
—THOMAS WATSON, SR.

CHAPTER 10

Humor Is Not Always Funny

An employee shows up late for work.
The boss yells, "You should have been here at 8:30!"
The employee replies, "Why? What happened at 8:30?"

A sense of humor is a valuable tool. Humor can disarm, build rapport, break the ice, and create interest in a discussion, speech, or any written communication. Humor can also be divisive, disruptive, offensive, ill timed, and overused. The jokes, pranks, riddles, and witty remarks you use among your friends may not play well in a business setting. What you heard on TV's evening talk shows and sitcoms may not be the best choice for your business interaction. It is important to understand the difference.

It is critical to abstain from humor that has the hint of damaging your professional reputation. If you think anyone could question your intent of a joke, don't tell it. It is not worth it to risk your reputation on a silly joke. Anything questionable, abstain.

The following are three major humor traps to avoid if you want to become Indispensable.

Humor Trap 1

There was this priest, rabbi, pastor, Democrat, and Republican in a boat ...

All political, religious, racial, sexual, and other types of targets of group-demeaning jokes, stories, or antidotes are the quicksand pools of the business world. You cannot be sure what side of the fence, what biases, or what emotional ties your audience may consider sensitive, serious, and not amusing. You thought you were on firm ground, having fun, and suddenly you are up to your neck in a bad situation. Even if you think you have a certain rapport with your business associates and even if they have already shared such a story with you, save such humor for your after-hours circle of friends.

You may think this is extreme. You are certain you have close friends at work who share your humor. You may have a joke that is simply too funny not to share, and so you do. Your business pals laugh and laugh. They cannot believe how funny you are. Why, they are so impressed that later they share it with others, using your name as the original source of the hilarious punch line. Suddenly there are others who are associating your name with the compromising tale, and one of those people takes offense. Maybe someone with an ax to grind, with you. Maybe someone who believes HR would be interested in such a story. And there you are in HR, alone ... no pals, no laughs, no Tarzan.

Humor Trap 2

Nothing is funnier than a good impersonation. There are comedians who become rich and famous because they can some-how mimic the looks and mannerisms of certain individuals.

But the goal of the impersonator is to make fun of the subject, not revere them. We laugh because the comedian exaggerates the target's humanity, errors, and habits. We know the joke is at the victim's expense, but the ridicule is simply too funny not to enjoy.

In the 1990s, Dana Carvey made the nation laugh with his impersonation of President George H. W. Bush. We tuned in and waited as Mr. Carvey worked through the script to get to his famous phrase "wouldn't be prudent." We laughed and joined in with our friends whenever the moment or circumstances would allow "wouldn't be prudent." Who knows if the president ever uttered those words? Who knows if the president cared? But Mr. Carvey struck gold with his mocking impersonation.

It may be fun and laughable to us, but does the target enjoy the humorous attack? Does the target have a choice? Would it be fun and laughable if you were the target? Once? Daily?

As humans, we all have quirks, physical challenges, favorite sayings, and distinctive physical attributes. Some of them are hilarious ... to others. It becomes very tempting to identify those traits our coworkers have, especially our bosses. If you are willing to offer quick impersonations of others, your work friends may well find you side-splittingly hilarious. They may ask you to perform it over and over. They will be clueless as to why you are not headlining in Vegas. They may attempt to join you in the skit. They may well suggest that you perform to other employees. You are indeed very entertaining, at a noncompensated level.

But what if the targets see or hear? Even if they too smile on the outside, what is the feeling on the inside? The reality is, you are mocking them. You are funny at their expense. Perhaps it is seemingly harmless. Perhaps you feel it is all in good fun. But your entertainment skill set may also be dangerous to your reputation, business standing, and future. Even in the entertainment world, comedians are not often considered serious actors. We are conditioned to laugh at them but not necessarily believe them.

Humor Trap 3

Negative humor. You know it when you hear it. It is that shot, that jab, that seemingly playful retort that may be funny but takes a direct shot at someone. Yes, it is something you may "give and take" with your friends. Such banters are fun and accepted among folks who have a common bond, long-term relationship, or a shared appreciation. When you toss such humor at people you trust, it is usually understood as playful. When it is in a business setting, you may be creating an adversary. Your targets may feel embarrassed or disrespected. Yes, it may have been funny; yes, it may have seemed innocent; and yes, you may have counterpunched a shot that was aimed at you. But negative humor in a business setting is dangerous.

"The Comeback" was an episode in the highly successful *Seinfeld* TV show. One of the storylines in "The Comeback" episode included George Costanza passionately eating shrimp during a meeting while he was employed by the New York Yankees. One of his coworkers, Reilly, takes the opportunity to lob a shot at George in front of their mutual coworkers during a meeting. Reilly says, "Hey, George, the ocean called. They are running out of shrimp."

All the other coworkers laughed and laughed with great amusement. George took offense at being embarrassed in front of his coworkers, even though he truly was eating the shrimp in an obsessive manner. He began plotting a counterpunch, a comeback. He planned to set up a similar scenario and then pound Reilly with the following line: "Well, the jerk store called, and they're running out of you!"

Jerry, Elaine, and Kramer all attempted to persuade George that his cherished line was not funny. They offered alternative lines. Jerry suggested, "The zoo called, and you're due back at six." But George was confident in his retort. As George's plans reached deployment, Reilly was released by the Yankees and took a job in Ohio working for Firestone. Disappointed that he would never have the opportunity to even the score, George set up a bogus meeting with Firestone, and he traveled from New York all the way to Ohio just to be in front of Reilly. George managed to set up the situation as desired and confidently deployed his jerk store line. Sadly, no one thought the zinger was funny, and George was embarrassed yet a second time.

Seinfeld was a sitcom, but the message is valid. If you choose to embarrass people in front of their peers, no matter how funny, you may well compromise trusted relationships and develop a rivalry. Revenge is a powerful emotion. Retaliation knows no calendar and is often "ramped up" in its release. Better for you to refrain from the original zinger, no matter how enticing the circumstances. Negative humor is risky … funny, but risky.

So if you can't use politically incorrect or sensitive material, impersonations, or negative humor, what humor is left?

There are a zillion good jokes and stories. You have experienced events in your life that are funny. You can have some fun with a department at your work, provided you are part of that department. You can make light of the human experience (provided it is not off color). And you can always make fun of yourself, provided it is not a consistent subject matter.

I went to the psychiatrist, and he says,
"You're crazy."
I tell him I want a second opinion.
He says, "Okay, you're ugly too!"
—RODNEY DANGERFIELD

If you target something about yourself consistently, others will join in, expecting it is OK with you. Let's say you are hair challenged. Most folks have the decency not to walk up and start laughing at your receding hairline. However, if you start consistently making fun of your own head, others will follow your lead. Maybe this is OK with you, but be aware it likely will not dissipate on its own.

The important thing is take time to LAUGH! Some say laughing cures diseases, reduces stress, and lowers blood pressure. Enjoy who you are, enjoy who you know, and enjoy what you have. Laugh. Don't take yourself too seriously. Laugh. Understand that when someone you know hurts your feelings, it is more often than not, unintentional. Laugh. Sometimes you embarrass yourself. Laugh. Life is short and trouble will come. Laugh. You will be respected, honored, appreciated, revered, and admired because you laughed. You will disarm the aggressive, ease the tense, and find common ground. Laugh.

Take Action

- Stop and laugh. Most people are way too serious, and it really will not matter in a hundred years. Don't be afraid to laugh at yourself. Laughter is contagious—spread it around your workplace.

- Eliminate all jokes that could compromise your reputation ... period.

- Never use humor that ridicules others unless you are in that group, no matter how funny it would be.

- Don't take yourself too seriously. No one else does.

The Indispensable person has a great sense of humor but guards it wisely.

CHAPTER 11

Business Is Business

Eat and drink with your relatives;
do business with strangers.
—GREEK PROVERB

You have been invited to a business lunch at one of the best restaurants in town. Upper management will be there, an important client will be there, and many of your peers will attend.

As you enter the restaurant, you are immediately greeted with honor by the establishment's staff, and you are led to the table. This is a rare event indeed. The elegance and ambiance of this restaurant surpass the typical dining spots you frequent. There are more glasses and utensils by your charger plate than you use in a week. You attempt to look refined and select your seat as those around do so as well.

A well-dressed host grabs your napkin and folds it into a triangle and lays it in your lap. In the same smooth motion, he graciously offers you the menu. You glance around at the attendees to make sure your manners are consistent with theirs. Opening the menu, you see delicacies that you have longed to try. There listed within the beef selections is tenderloin of Kobe beef. Options from the sea include lobster tail fresh from Maine. The international section recommends the lamb flown in from New Zealand.

This indeed is your day! Now you get to live like the "others" do. It's your rare opportunity to dine like a king without the associated king's ransom. Suddenly you feel someone standing over your shoulder. It is the table attendant, there to take your order. "Oh, why not," you say to yourself. "Yes, I will take the ..."

*   *   *

Your organization's annual holiday celebration is taking place in a fabulous ballroom of a five-star hotel. There will be a live band, your friends, and an elaborate buffet. Oh, and there will be an open and fully stocked bar.

You arrive with great expectation. You are dressed as if the red carpet were your runway! The evening proceeds spectacularly. Upper management is there, and you have the opportunity to visit with them and their spouses. Some even call you by name. You, my friend, are moving up. You engage the attendees, hang out with your friends, and exchange holiday pleasantries.

Over the speaker system there is a strange tapping followed by an electronic squeal. You turn to see the company president standing at a microphone. The president thanks everyone for attending and then reports that the company has had record profits. Everyone will be receiving a 10 percent end-of-year bonus! The crowd erupts with celebration. With that, the president exits the stage and returns to the crowd. You turn to your friends and extend your hand for the high-five slap ... PARTEEEE TIME! You have earned this celebration. The open bar means FREE beverages, and now the real celebration can begin ... because free is good!

After an hour or so, you have visited the bartender multiple times. The friends at your table seem to be laughing at you, but you are not sure why. It suddenly dawns on you. There are some things you have wanted to say and scores to settle with some of your fellow employees. Somehow this seems like the right time. You even have a couple of ideas to float by upper management. Grabbing your near-empty glass you swerve toward ...

*　*　*

Business is business.

Webster's dictionary defines *business* as "the buying and selling of commodities and services and connotes a profit motive." [1]

The simple truth is, businesses that are not successful do not remain businesses for long. A successful business must meet a need and deliver products or services, whatever they may be, profitably. When entrepreneurs, business owners, or managers look to hire people to assist with the products or services associated with that business, they are hoping to find people who will assist in the success of the company, not the demise.

Webster's dictionary describes an *employee* as a person hired to work for wages or salary. Simply a worker who is hired to perform a job.[2]

So let the mistrust begin.

Most of your fellow employees do not share the company's goals, brand, or even the desire for the company's ultimate success. They probably don't invest their energy understanding the vision, the objectives, or the multiyear plan of the organization.

Many do not consider that their actions, habits, and activities affect the overall financial success of the organization. They consider their positions as a daily drudgery rather than as a lasting opportunity. Most of them feel entitled rather than appreciative for their position. Almost all employees feel undervalued.

Do some employers disrespect, mistreat, exploit, and underappreciate their employees? Absolutely! But consider the U.S. Department of Commerce's statistics suggesting that over 75 percent of employees steal from their employers.[3] So businesses have learned to watch and expect that those they hire may not have the best intentions.

This is great news for you! All those people around you may not have the best intent or be giving their best effort to the business at hand.

Instead of considering yourself an employee, what if you considered yourself an ambassador of your employer? Webster's dictionary defines *ambassador* as "a person skilled in dealing with other people; tactful person."[4] A diplomatic agent is considered of high rank and ability.

What if you considered yourself as a diplomat for your organization of the highest rank? What if you performed your tasks as if you represented the brand, the strategies, and the financially profitable goals of your employer? The title on your business card may not immediately reflect any change. The numbers on your paycheck may not increase in the short term. But do you think it would help you become indispensable? Of course it would.

So how do you go from employee to ambassador? Here are some ideas.

A Change of Attitude

You may think your employer, circumstances, and pressures are holding you back. You may think the entire world is against you. And if you believe this is so, then you are right. You are right because the most important, the most influential, the most crucial person in your path has been convinced. That would be you.

You are in charge of your future. Yes, there are obstacles, troubles, hurdles, concerns, illnesses, and hardships, both today and in the future. And as long as you draw breath, there are solutions, actions, activities, efforts, plans, and strategies that you can deploy to defeat those issues. You can wake up angry at the day, or you can wake up feeling blessed and happy. You can feel discouraged, or you can take action. You can feel everyone is against you, or you can feel determined to overcome. You can droop your shoulders like a victim, or you can swagger like a victor.

It is easier to feel afraid than courageous. It is easier to quit than fight on. It is easier to blame others rather than ourselves. Remember, the easy way out does not often end in celebration, recognition, or reward. Where you are today has no authority over where you could be in the future.

Your attitude is a magnet. You attract others who have the same attitudes.

Positive attitudes make us happier, more productive, and more successful—few people would disagree. Then, why would anyone in the world choose negativism—a self-inflicted wound—and all the ramifications that come along with that choice? Why would people choose to hurt themselves by being negative? Maybe they choose to be negative because they don't realize they have the power to be positive ... or perhaps they enjoy feeling sorry for themselves ... or it is more difficult to be positive.

I think it is because negative attitudes are a natural response ... and some people enjoy it. They say they are being "realistic," which in most cases means exposing the negative and cynical response to a situation ... refusing to even acknowledge the "just as realistic" positive response.

The Indispensable people choose not to inflict the poison of negative attitudes on themselves. Instead, they choose to be positive and enthusiastic. They add energy to those around them. Negative and cynical people zap the energy from those around them.

When was the last time you knew a successful person who people consistently described as "negative" and "cynical"? In my years of experience, I cannot name one successful person described that way. Not one.

Coincidental? I don't think so. Optimism and enthusiasm are two traits that you will find in the best employees and leaders, regardless of industry, profession, or age.

The power of enthusiasm is evidenced by the effect it has on other people. We have all witnessed the enthusiastic school kids selling candy door-to-door. They are enthusiastic because they are confident in themselves, love their product, and enjoy achieving a goal. We are happy to buy from them.

We have also witnessed kids who are trying to sell candy just because that is what they have to do. There is no passion, enthusiasm, or energy. The candy is the same, the customers are the same, yet the sales are not even close. The missing ingredient is enthusiasm.

Real enthusiasm and a positive attitude are not things you put on or take off to fit the occasion or to impress people. Real enthusiasm is a way of life. Yet many people allow conditions to control their attitude rather than allowing their attitude to help control conditions.

A positive attitude is at least as important as how we dress, look, hone our skills, or add to our education, and it is at least as important as how gifted we think we are. You control your attitude. Make sure it is worth catching.

BECOME A MENTOR AND TEACHER

There's a Chinese proverb that says, "If you continually give, you will continually have." We all know that the more you give, the more you will receive, but that is not the reason you give. You give so that you will have more opportunities to give. And, you will ultimately receive what you have given. Let that soak in—you will ultimately receive what you have given. If you give encouragement, help, hope, knowledge, and support, you will ultimately receive encouragement, help, hope, knowledge, and support when you need it. If you give hate, fear, doubt, harsh criticism, then when you need help, there will not be many, if any, people in line to lend a hand. You will get what you have given.

Not long ago, I heard of a man who lost his home in a fire. Everything was gone up in smoke in minutes. It was devastating ... years of possessions destroyed. When asked about the fire, he said that what he came to realize was that the things he had given away were still available to him while the things he had held on to were gone forever. What a great life lesson. What you give away, you will always have access to. What you keep, you can lose within minutes.

The Indispensable person gives away knowledge by sharing it with others. As a side benefit, the more you teach, the more committed you become to what you are teaching. Find people who are interested in your field of expertise, and teach them how to become better. And as you teach others, you will be able to hone and update your skills. Give your knowledge away, and you will become more knowledgeable!

Focus on displaying cheerfulness, cooperation, gratitude, and eagerness. Smile at people! Tell people they had a good idea. Tell people you appreciate them. Make others feel valuable, regardless of who they are, what they do, or what their status is. Acknowledge them for their value to the organization. In a world of stone-faced, grumpy, bored, zombiefied people, you will stand out. Give it a try!

If you accept your self-appointed new role and title as Ambassador at the Highest Rank, your views and actions will change. Even more, other people's view of you will change.

BUSINESS MEALS ARE ABOUT BUSINESS, NOT ABOUT EATING

There are occasions when you may find yourself as a participant in a business outing that includes a lunch or dinner. The meal may include customers, potential clients, coworkers, and/or managers. It could be a celebration, an ongoing negotiation, or a chance to work out some issues. Whichever the restaurant, whatever the delicacies served, and even if the chef is of great renown, the last thing you need to do is to consider it lunch or dinner. You need to think business first!

While dining with business associates, use all the manners you have been taught, and if you are unsure of anything, mirror someone you consider more experienced. General rules are forks to the left, knives to the right, dessert cutlery at the top, bread and butter plate top left, glasses to the top right. Place your napkin folded triangularly (keeps it more secure) in your lap, keep your elbows off the table, and never be the first to begin eating.

When the menu arrives, check with others for a recommendation and what they are planning to order. Try not to be the first to order. Should the waiter ask you first, you could say that you have not decided and suggest he begin with another guest. The reason is that you do not want to order the filet if everyone else is having chicken salad. You want to order a meal that is comparable to what the others at the table are ordering.

Try to abstain from any food that could create a splash. This would include foods like spaghetti, ribs, and anything you have to open or shell. Beware of small tomatoes, which could spew juice. Stay away from foods you eat with your hands.

Consider the risk of ordering green. Of course your mother spent years telling you to eat green vegetables. But what if you are involved in an important conversation during dinner, unaware that your fellow guests are wondering whether to mention the spinach lodged between your teeth.

Slow down. Never begin eating until all of the guests at your table have received their servings. Pace yourself … don't be the first finished.

Business meals are not always about discussing business. However, treat every business meal as business—everything counts.

OFFICE PARTIES

Understand that office parties, even those after hours, are really still business functions.

Yes, indeed, HR rules are still in force, management hierarchy is still in order, and your reputation can still be tainted. The open bar may offer you $50 of free beverages and $1,000s less in potential income, should you lose your decorum. Your future and business reputation are better served by keeping your party animal caged during a business affair. Any actions, discussions, and/or confrontations while adult beverages are being served could lead to undesired HR interaction.

REMOVE YOURSELF FROM THE COMPLAINERS

You know who they are. They hang together, go on break together, and spew it out together. They complain, they degrade, they gossip, they accuse, they tear down, they dislike, and they feel like "corporate and/or the world" are all against them.

Don't participate. Run!

Your organization may have problems—name one that doesn't. It may need changes in management, policies, brand, compensation, and procedures, and it may have a variety of issues. But what positive actions will be deployed from a group of employees whose favorite pastime is to complain and gossip about others? What will happen is that you will be identified as someone who participates in, agrees with, and cooperates with negative sentiment. Others in your company may choose not to trust you because they KNOW about that group of complainers.

> *Tell me your friends, and I'll tell you who you are.*
> —Assyrian Proverb

Refuse to degrade anything or anyone in such a forum. Strive toward positive change. If there are issues in your company that need improvement, work through proper channels to address change. If there are misconceptions between departments, suggest interaction and discussion between those groups to problem-solve rather than amplify.

Be Conscientious with Time

Get to work early enough to be ready to begin on time. Yes, there may be traffic issues and other unforeseen obstacles that may result in occasional tardiness. But being late every day due to associated issues is not really a valid excuse. It means you are leaving home too late.

It is one thing to show up on time. It is another to have your game face on and be ready to go! However much time, chatter, or coffee it takes, be ready to face it all as an ambassador when the workday begins!

When Things Get Tough

It is easy to become cynical and skeptical ... especially when things get tough. In fact, most people are that way. The Indispensable person understands that things are not always the way they should be. But he or she also has the courage to do something to improve the here and now.

I once knew an elderly lady whom I consider to be the wisest and most positive person I have ever known. She did not have much money, or formal education, nor did she work outside the home. Yet she had earned a PhD in common sense and wisdom.

She loved to teach her children, grandchildren, and the neighborhood kids life's principles by telling stories. One thing that would drive her a little crazy was how some people chose to see nothing but problems. They were blinded by their own issues in life, and they loved to tell others how miserable they were. She would tire quickly of listening to what she called their "bellyaching."

One of the nuggets of wisdom from this old friend that I will always remember is how to face problems and be positive, no matter what the situation.

She loved to tell the story of how a particular group of people would line up along the perimeter of a field about the size of a football field. While standing on the outskirts of the field, everyone would be given the opportunity to throw their problems onto the middle of the field. Once all the problems had been thrown and were covering the field, the people standing around the field would be given the chance to choose which ones to pick up and take home.

Most people would probably pick up their own problems and go back home, realizing that they really do not have it that bad.

You know, I think that she's right on the money with this story. So much of life is about how we handle what life throws our way. The Indispensable person knows that life is good—even when a situation appears to be the worst. But he or she also knows how to help make another's life better.

Take Action

- Every meal is business. Every open bar is business. Wherever you are, you have the opportunity to demonstrate that you are different—you are Indispensable!

- Even when you are having a bad day, you can be a positive person at work.

- Smile—every chance you get.

- Greet others with eagerness and friendliness.

- Your attitude is contagious and attracts others like a magnet.

- Stay away from negative groups and people. Don't let them drag you down.

The Indispensable person recognizes that no matter the occasion, business is business.

SECTION FIVE

That Was Then; This Is Now

When I let go of what I am, I become what I might be.
—Lao Tsu

CHAPTER 12

EAT More

If you wish to know the road up the mountain, ask
the man who goes back and forth on it.
—ZENRIN

C an you eat more and become indispensable? Sure, you
can—as long as you EAT the right stuff.

No, we're not talking more fruits, vegetables, and grains here.
The right stuff for anyone becoming indispensable is being an
eager learner who is *action oriented* and *thankful* for the opportunities
ahead—no matter what.

EAGER LEARNER

The Indispensable person is usually someone who has developed
an insatiable appetite for learning. He is eager to learn from his
own experiences, other people, and from the books he reads.

Do you think it is coincidental that, in most cases, the bigger the
house, the bigger the library inside the house? Check it out when

you visit other people's homes. See what kinds of books they have on their bookshelves. You can tell a lot about people by the books they read. Show me their library, and that library will show me their philosophy and values.

Chief executive officers of major organizations are said to read four books a month, yet most American workers do not read four books in a lifetime. That makes no sense to me. How could a CEO invest the time to read four books a month while the average employee will not read one book a year? No wonder the CEOs appear to have more knowledge. They do! But the knowledge they apply at work probably did not come from the knowledge they learned in college. It came from the exact same place you can get it—from a bookcase.

Most people say that they do not have the time to become eager learners. That is simply not true.

You can choose to be in the top 1 percent of all readers by reading a book each month. A book per month is about half a chapter a day, maybe 10 minutes. Be part of the top 1 percent for an investment of 10 minutes a day? What a deal! Think about it. If you read a book a month for one year, you would have read 12 books about your chosen field. In five years, you would have read 60! If you had read 60 books when your competitors for the job had read 3, don't you think that you would have a better chance to be indispensable for the job you are pursuing?

Your challenge is not finding the time. Your challenge is creating personal discipline. If you can develop the discipline to block off at least 10 minutes every day and devote that time to learning, it will separate you from competitors who are also pursuing the next opportunity.

The benefit is that the more you learn, the more you will be able to earn. You will become more valuable to your organization because of your knowledge. You are cheating yourself if you go through a day without learning something new.

The good news is that there is an abundance of books available to teach you or inform you about any subject you are interested in, and there is a direct correlation between the books you read and the success you achieve. Here's a challenge. Read one book that applies to your profession. Just one. You will find that learning is contagious and you will want to learn more.

A friend and wise counsel of mine always said, "You are today what you'll be five years from now, except for the people you meet and the books you read." Think about that. In five years, you can be completely different or just like you are right now. It is your choice.

ACTION ORIENTED

The Indispensable person is someone who has the courage to take action.

Through the years, I have seen hundreds of people who have had the talent, ability, and even the desire to move forward. Yet, because of their inability to take action, they became paralyzed. They waffled on decisions. Their values were constantly changing. And they were swayed by the latest political correctness.

I once saw a movie filmed in South Africa. Two families were killed, and only a boy and girl survived. While attempting to cross the Sahara, they came across a bushman. The bushman began to lead them across the Sahara, but about halfway across, the boy began to quit. He sat down and looked at the three tracks of footprints they had made as they walked across the desert. The bushman came up to him and said, "Unless that is your future, I would not focus on it for very long. You must focus on what you can control and then keep moving."

Don't let your past eat your future. When you focus on things outside your control, you lose control.

Taking action involves clearly defining your personal values and standing up for those values. Are you willing to take a risk to accomplish your goals? Are you willing to address negativity and resolve issues before they become bigger issues?

Remember: negativity, worry, and anger can shut down your ability to take action.

The Indispensable person is ready to take action, seize control, and move forward pursuing the issues and goals that really matter.

THANKFUL

OK, life is not always a bowl of cherries. But there is a profound truth in this Pollyanna attitude: look for the good, and you will find it. Look for the bad, and you will find it. It is your choice to make.

One person said that the only reason the grass always looks greener "over there" is because you are not there—and the people who live "over there" know how to hide the manure better. True or not, the more time you can spend looking to improve where you are, instead of looking where you think you should be, the more successful you will be.

I have seen hundreds of very talented people during my career who kept waiting, waiting, and waiting for the exact right time to dedicate themselves to improvement. They were stuck on "Someday Isle." Someday I'll be committed. Someday I'll begin to set goals. Someday I'll help others achieve their goals. They never escaped from the Someday Isle.

Someday Isle is full of good, honest people who are not willing to escape. The people on the isle keep looking for the perfect situation, which rarely comes to anyone on Someday Isle. The people who move forward and get ahead leave Someday Isle and do something every day to escape the comfort of Someday Isle. Don't be paralyzed by Someday Isle and wake up to see that your opportunity has passed!

Spending time improving where you are, instead of looking where you think you should be, is the key to escaping Someday Isle.

A friend of mine is a sports psychologist who works with several professional golfers. He says that in every round of golf, there are three or four things that are going to happen that are not deserved. You may hit a ball in the middle of the fairway, and it lands in a sand divot. Or as soon as you hit, the wind gusts up sending your well-struck ball into the bunker in front of the green. Or you may hit a sprinkler head that sends the ball into the rough. Three or four undeserved "somethings" will happen. He says that what separates the champions in golf is how they react to those undeserved situations.

Becoming indispensable at work is no different. The question is not, "Are things going to happen that you do not deserve?" Of course they will. Look for them, and work through them. The unknown question is, "How will you react?"

Do you react like a champion and focus on the future? Or do you focus on whom to blame for the situation you are now facing?

The Indispensable person learns to be thankful, "no matter what," by focusing on where she is—not on where she thinks she should be. Focus on the facts of your situation, take control, and accept responsibility to make it better.

Take Action

- Read at least one nonfiction book per month that will help you in your career.

- Start a book club at work—learning will become contagious.

- Confront negativity, and take action for improvement.

- Focus on making things better, no matter what circumstances come along.

The Indispensable person is an eager learner, action oriented, and thankful for the opportunities ahead.

CHAPTER 13

Your Move

*Many of life's failures are people who did not realize
how close they were to success when they gave up.*
—THOMAS EDISON

Governmental agencies and polling firms study average
Americans—what they earn, how much school they have
completed, how much TV they watch, how much money they
have in the bank, and so on. *Average* means common, every day,
run-of-the-mill, usual, general, and ordinary. The polling firms are
expecting you to be that type person.

Skew the average! You are different from anyone who has ever walked
this earth. You are average only if you allow yourself to be average.
You have authority over your emotions, actions, ambitions, and
future. You do not have to accept and settle for status quo. You need
not succumb to being a victim of circumstances. Take charge of your
goals and your life. Be determined. You do not have to be average.

What are you doing to increase your knowledge and capabilities?
Many people spend too many hours watching TV, playing games,

accumulating electronic correspondence, and notifying others of their piddling. What if you determined to be much more than average? What if you spent half of your "entertainment time" reading something instructional, taking an online course to enhance your computing skills, participating in ongoing education courses or groups, and planning your strategies for tomorrow? You would increase your value.

You would no longer be average. You would be Indispensable.

What if you took authority over your emotions and responses? What if you woke up and determined to exude joy and happiness? What if you assumed a can-do attitude rather than a gloom-and-doom mentality? What if you smiled at people you did not know and complimented them on something? What if you did not allow selfish people access to your emotions? What if you counted 10 things every day for which you were thankful, rather than grumbling about what you don't have? What if you told your spouse, your children, your significant other, your parents, and your dear friends that you loved them? What if you told them you were proud of them? Your life would change.

You would no longer be average. You would be Indispensable.

What if you took control over what influences your life? What if you looked in the mirror and demanded more of the occupant? What if you said that excuses were done? What if you took control of what you ate, what you drank, what you allowed to captivate your body and mind? What if you proclaimed that fear, anxiety, and insecurity are not the boss of you? What if you did not allow any individual to compromise who you are and where you are going? What if you established goals and jealously set a path to achieve them?

You would no longer be average. You would be Indispensable.

It is your move. It is your life. Live it.

Require the best of yourself. Rebrand yourself. Look, practice, and perform the part. Continue to learn and grow in ability and capability. Eliminate any thought of entitlement and focus on bringing value. Refuse to give fear, insecurity, and any thoughts of surrender access to your goals. Recognize where there is turmoil, there is opportunity. Take guarded ownership of your emotions and actions. Laugh, love, find passion, be thankful, and encourage others. Be loyal to those who trust you. This is your life, your time, your watch. Be fierce. Increase your value.

The Indispensable person accepts that the next move is always his or her move. No excuses or justifications for why things are the way they are. It is your time to move forward.

CHAPTER 14

Back to the Future

At a location near you. Six months from today.

You have been called to attend a mandatory organization meeting. There is apprehension, excitement, and speculation about why the meeting was called. The entire organization has been asked to participate either in person or on a conference call, a highly unusual request.

Rumors are rampant. Is the organization merging with a competitor? Is it being sold? Will there be layoffs? Are we unveiling a top-secret new product line? Is the CEO stepping down?

The bottom line is that no one knows the purpose of the meeting. Everyone knows for sure that they're in for some BIG NEWS.

The president and CEO arrive with board members in tow. You can tell they've been burning the midnight oil. Their usually perfectly creased pants and starched shirts look slept in. There are bags under their eyes. But they also look really excited and seem to be all smiles.

After the usual pleasantries and logistics to ensure that all conference callers are hooked up properly, the president begins the announcement:

> For the past several years, our organization has continued to impress our customers and the investment community with our performance. We are the proven leader in our field—both in quality and service. Our market share has skyrocketed. Our employees are the best the industry has to offer. We've compiled an impressive list of accomplishments in a relatively short time.
>
> But today we are here to take our organization—and you—to the next level. Last night, our board of directors gave final approval to an aggressive expansion strategy. Our plans are to expand our product offerings and our geographic presence. We will become an international organization with new offices in Mexico, Canada, and Europe. We're also planning to open offices in four major cities around the United States.
>
> These are exciting—but challenging—times for us. Our greatest task is to get the right people into the right places to lead this aggressive expansion. I know many of you have been preparing for opportunities to advance with our organization. That time is now. We will immediately begin our search for leaders who are willing to accept these new challenges.
>
> Thanks to each of you for your contributions to our unprecedented success. Our vice president of human resources will now outline the interviewing and selection process for these exciting new opportunities.

The silence that follows is deafening. This is awesome news, but it is totally unexpected. What are the new opportunities? Who will be considered?

Answering a few questions, the president and CEO then leave the room to exuberant applause and a standing ovation.

Many have not prepared. Many were surprised. Many have been disengaged.

You?

You confidently smile because you have become … the indispensable, obvious choice!!

$$* \quad * \quad *$$

May life's journey bring you success, happiness, balance to your life, and a clear vision of the opportunities presented to you, as you become the Indispensable choice for your next opportunity.

Notes

CHAPTER 1

1. Resource: http://www.gallup.com/poll/150383/Majority-American-Workers-Not-Engaged-Jobs.aspx.

CHAPTER 4

1. Resource: http://www.psychologicalscience.org/onlyhuman/2006/07/velocity-of-trust.cfm.

CHAPTER 5

1. Resource: http://thehiringsite.careerbuilder.com/2011/07/06/do-clothes-make-the-manager-employers-weigh-in/.

2. Source: Valerie Sokolosky, *Do It Right:* The New Book of *Business Etiquette,* CornerStone Leadership Institute, Dallas, TX, 2007.

CHAPTER 7

1. Source: Adapted from Drs. Kathlyn and Gay Hendricks, *Attracting Genuine Love*, Sounds True, Boulder, CO, 2004.

CHAPTER 8

1. Source: David Cottrell and Tony Jeary, *136 Effective Presentation Tips*, CornerStone Leadership Institute, Dallas, TX, 2008.

CHAPTER 11

1. Resource: *Webster's New World College Dictionary*, Fourth Edition, Wiley Publishing, Inc., Cleveland, OH, 2010.

2. Ibid.

3. Employee theft: http://www.cbsnews.com/8301-505143_162-48640192/employee-theft-are-you-blind-to-it/

4. Resource: *Webster's New World College Dictionary*, Fourth Edition.

Acknowledgments

Thank you for investing your time with us by reading this book. We have offered insights from loving parents, experienced managers, and wise mentors. In some cases, our mistakes and embarrassing moments have been our best instructors.

I am confident that the suggestions provided in *Indispensable!* will help you reach your goals and aspirations. Please let me know about your success in becoming Indispensable! I would love to hear from you. Write me at Robert@CornerStoneLeadership.com.

David and I would like to thank the CornerStone team, our 24,000 customers who have remained loyal to CornerStone Leadership Institute for the past 17 years, and the team at McGraw-Hill led by Knox Huston. Please accept our deepest gratitude.

We are especially grateful to our families who have been our rock during both great and challenging times. They are our treasure and inspiration.

Without a doubt, I am blessed. I thank God every day for allowing me the opportunity to live this day.

Robert Nix
Midlothian, Texas

Three Ways to Bring
Indispensable! into Your
Organization

1. **The *Indispensable!* PowerPoint™ Presentation**
   Introduce and reinforce *Indispensable!* to your organization
   with this cost-effective, downloadable PowerPoint™
   presentation. Includes a facilitator guide and notes. $99.95
   Downloadable from www.CornerStoneLeadership.com

2. **Keynote Presentation**
   Invite author Robert Nix or David Cottrell to inspire your
   team and help create greater success for your organization.
   Each presentation is designed to set a solid foundation for
   both organizational and personal success.
   Contact Michele@CornerStoneLeadership.com

3. **The *Indispensable!* Workshop**
   Facilitated by Robert Nix or a certified CornerStone
   Leadership instructor, this three- or six-hour workshop will
   reinforce the principles of *Indispensable!* Each participant will
   develop a personal action plan that can make a profound
   difference in his or her life and career.
   Contact Michele@CornerStoneLeadership.com

Recommended Resources
for Additional Study

Monday Morning Choices: 12 Powerful Ways to Go from Ordinary to Extraordinary

Tuesday Morning Coaching: 8 Simple Truths to Boost Your Career and Your Life

Orchestrating Attitude: Getting the Best from Yourself and Others

You Gotta Get in the Game: How to Win in Business, Sales, and Life

Do It Right: The New Book of Business Etiquette

The Eight Constants of Change: What Leaders Need to Know to Drive Change and Win

TIME! 105 Ways to Get More Done Every Workday

Winners Always Quit: 7 Pretty Good Habits You Can Swap for Really Great Results

136 Effective Presentation Tips: Inspire, Inform, and Influence Anyone, Anywhere, Anytime

All recommended resources available at
www.CornerStoneLeadership.com

Indispensable! Package

All the books listed on the previous page plus
Indispensable! and *David Cottrell's Collection of Favorite Quotations*
$129.95!
That's a savings of 35 percent!

About the Authors

David Cottrell, president and CEO of CornerStone Leadership Institute, is an internationally known leadership consultant, educator, and speaker. His business experience includes leadership positions with Xerox and FedEx. He also led the successful turnaround of a chapter 11 company before founding CornerStone.

He is the author of more than 25 books, including *Monday Morning Mentoring, Monday Morning Choices, Listen Up, Leader, Monday Morning Motivation, Tuesday Morning Coaching,* and *The Magic Question*.

David is a thought-provoking and electrifying professional speaker. He has presented his leadership message to over 300,000 managers worldwide. His powerful wisdom and insights on leadership have made him a highly sought after keynote speaker and seminar leader.

David can be reached at David@CornerStoneLeadership.com.

Robert Nix is a dynamic salesman, speaker, and author. He has been successful in sales and sales management for over 30 years, and he has represented software, technology, and transaction processing companies to many of the largest businesses in America.

Robert's incredible creativity and his ability to speak and to teach are his gifts and passions. He is also the author of *The Adventures of Jake Palestine, P.I., in the Case of the Empty Tomb*.

Robert brings a creative, energetic, and challenging style to presentations and conferences. He can be reached at Robert@CornerStoneLeadership.com.